I0749787

IF YOU CAN HEAR THIS

Poems in Protest of an American Inauguration

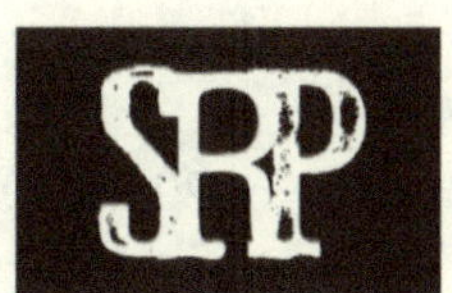

SIBLING RIVALRY PRESS
LITTLE ROCK, ARKANSAS
DISTURB / ENRAPTURE

If You Can Hear This:
Poems in Protest of an American Inauguration

This anthology is published and distributed as Issue 25 of *Assaracus: A Journal of Gay Poetry.*

Edited by Bryan Borland

Cover art: "Fallen Progress" by Seth Ruggles Hiler, commissioned specifically for this anthology. Cover design by Seth Pennington of Sibling Rivalry Press.

Sibling Rivalry Press, LLC
PO Box 26147
Little Rock, AR 72221

info@siblingrivalrypress.com
www.siblingrivalrypress.com

ISBN: 978-1943977-34-5
Assaracus ISSN: 2159-0478
Library of Congress Control No: 2017930182

This title is housed permanently in the Rare Books and Special Collections Vault of the Library of Congress.

First Sibling Rivalry Press Edition, January 2017

IF YOU CAN HEAR THIS

We're half-awake in a fake empire

—The National

Bryan Borland

IF YOU CAN HEAR THIS

If you can hear this

    you are the resistance
    you are the underground

there is static in the air

the connection isn't stable
there is talk   no longer rumor
of iron walls and white curtains

but if you can hear this
    you are the resistance

get the books you love
you'll need them more than ever
harden your right to memory
you'll need that too
steel your body for the poison
and the antidote
if not bread and water
we must talk in the language
of poetry and survival

if you can hear this
    you understand

we now must decide what to fight
to protect first
who to hold closest
who to hide

whether to leave the art hanging
in the living room
or bury it for preservation

Nickole Brown

TRUMP'S TIC TACS

"I better use some Tic Tacs just in case I start kissing her.... I just start kissing them. It's like a magnet. Just kiss. I don't even wait. And when you're a star, they let you do it. You can do anything."

The night after my country loaded you
into its chamber and cocked
that long gun aimed straight for my
home, my wife and I were stuck
in a nearly dystopian line of unmoving
traffic. And because sugar comforts her
she popped those half-calorie candies
into her mouth and was bound to eat
the whole box herself until she shook out
from that hard plastic case the oranges ones,
just for me.

You see, Donald, this good woman,
she loves me. And she knows how the taste
of artificial orange makes me feel—
safe—makes me remember fevers broken
by the chalk tangerine of baby aspirin,
cool rags upon me, and a soft knock
on my door saying, *Baby, don't get up;*
mama's just checking on you again.
That was back when another man
not so unlike you was insecure enough
to also think it best to freshen himself before
grabbing at me, and to this day
I don't remember much except: *Don't worry.*
I took a shower; it's clean.

Donald, the news coming through the radio
made me sick. We had to turn it off.
We drove in stand-still, bumper-to-bumper
silence, unable to speak, especially not

of you. Yet there you still were,
a rattling under my tongue—those three orange
candies, now tiny bullets, pills with a powdery zest
that never really were tasty but just mindless, addictive
in that high chemical way, not doing a damn thing
to sweeten anyone's breath. I could not spit
and could not swallow and helpless
let it dissolve in my mouth.

Robert Andrew Perez

IN AMERICA

too long; didn't reckon.
america is a novel so long america didn't read it.

america hates its face so much it holds a flag up to it when he shaves.
did i mention america is male.

america didn't ask for permission.

your america is so white, it's red.

you're america. no you're america.

/

re: america

dear america,

die, america.

love, america

sincere condolences
sincerely, america

/

america just stood there and watched.
america held the camera.
america threw the first stone.
truth or dare, america.
america dared me. double-dog dared me.
truth, america.

america is a novel written in english.

america won't relinquish the rights to/for translation.

america stopped writing.
last thought was, it's your fault.

go hug your uncle america.
america or else.

/

am(nesia)erica, amirite.

/

america the beautiful.
land that i love.
land of the brave.
home of the free.
remember the alamo.
never forget.
stronger together.
yes we can.
make america great again.
grab them by the pussy.
make america gay again.
make america grab again.
america was never great.
forget america.
america forgets.
american pie.
american pussy.
american horror story.
make america stronger.
stronger pussy.
make america together again.
yes forget america.
remember the pussy.
home of america.
beautiful the america.

america that i love.
grab america.
free america.
never make america.
make america remember.

Michael Klein

THE SCRIM

The burned-through scrim of a layer of consciousness.

The new reality. Discharged.

The country conspires every morning with morning news.

People don't see other people live.

We aren't reporting anymore what happened yesterday.

With science fiction and barely any technique, we are already

living in the future. Stunned. Burned. It's what we grieve: the

non-negotiable force of being stunned; who we imagined, who we could

never *fully* imagine: this magical thought: *becoming*.

The world tilts with the sea: the beautiful sea inside the sea: and

we thought: for a time: we could feel it.

Candice M. Kelsey

THE BIRTH OF PRESIDENT DONALD TRUMP
after Mary Shelley

By the hazy glistening light of the November moon,
as it crept inside, stumbling a bit
and tearing the curtains, I beheld the ugliest, animated mess
of discolored flesh—a wretched monster
whom this nation had created.
He sat down, straightened his silk tie, and pointed
toward me with a corpse-finger.
His mouth was moving, a malevolent grin
uttering folderol of bloat and gloat
like shifting alpine glaciers.
Perhaps he meant to thank us; I do not know,
but one of his eyes was fixed on his own reflection in the window pane.
He seemed detained by his own existence,
and as I rushed out the front door to escape, I saw
the echo of fiery torches and heard
the neighbors spark, *It's an early Christmas!*

Brad Richard

MAKING IT GREAT AGAIN

Yesterday was *amazing*. Remember? The sky bled,
so we took a picture, added cloud-bandages,
and captioned it "me saving the sky ☺."
The lilies of the vacant lot were choking
on their own vomit, so we took a picture:
"I ♥ lilies ☹." It felt good to be doing something.
It felt good to be saying we felt something.
Then our lamps and streetlights, our phones
and laptops started choking on their vomit,
and darkness slimed. Through the goo, we watched
video of the good old days—not ours, I guess,
but still, nice to see nice people smiling
over a man who fell black on his head, and police
whitely walking a girl to school while crowds cheered.
Today, we'd have to shoot her. Did I say that?
Sorry, I meant we love one another so much.
Too much, maybe. Gives me a headache. My head
hurts, where is it? Who has it? Who stole it
and dropped it in this septic tank in this
unclean bed where it saw things and tasted
all the uncleanness all your uncleanness
it was you it was you it was you—

Tomorrow's gonna be *amazing*. Wait and see.

John Andrews

ON DANCING IN SHACKLES

An infomercial sold my mother
wearable weights, tan with blue

Velcro, and that satisfying sound
familiar like paper ripped length-

wise, and I wore them for fun

playing Clydesdale or prisoner or
sand-bag around the house.
She was high kicking with extra

weight, accompanied by synth
and women working on their buns of steel,
VHS rolling like it was her

job, or dragging a wagon of horse shit
through nine acres of knee-high hay,
or pulling her child out of a pool

and snapping a water moccasin's neck
with the blunt blade of a shovel,
she never acknowledged the weights.

No matter how long loosed, the canvas
map still wrapped skin tight, despite
being unbound. It was unbearable,

pointless exercise. She only took them off
at night. And yet every morning,

tied them back on and even

with the memory of lightness fresh in her bones,
stepped higher than the day before.

Carl Napolitano

LEARNING TO STOP GLACIERS

When Olga leads me into the walk-in cooler
on my first day at work, opens a five-gallon tub of
cheese dip, and tips it sideways toward her,

the thick sticky white pours out slow, inching
over the edge, folding onto itself
in the metal serving container below,

as a glacier might slide across a frigid landscape,
scraping stone, pooling massively, hurdling
slowly with its muffled momentum for miles,

unstoppable.

But when the metal container fills,
Olga tips the bucket back up, and
with a gloved hand, runs her fingers
with swiftness and ease over the rim,
cutting the glacier in two—separating
what will be eaten soon from
what remains to be eaten later.

She peels the glove off and looks up at me
to see if I understand, if I know
what must be done, how it is best done.

This is how she teaches me: doing while I watch
(her English not good, my Spanish nonexistent).

This is what she teaches me:
how the world becomes large when we give it our full attention
but our hands become large too when we move them with purpose.

And while I shiver above her and nod my head,
I do not know if I will ever possess such grace.

Jessica Jacobs

NOVEMBER 9, 2016

Last summer, for the first time in eighty years,
June's full moon—that strawberry, honey,

planting moon—rose to meet
the summer solstice: the day of greatest light

bound to the night of greatest light
for the only time

in our lifetime. So after dinner and dancing,
we stepped naked into the sea

where my wife fit her body to mine,
making a shivering throne of my thighs.

Whatever lurked those waters, we turned
toward the sky, toward the light's

soft falling on the waves, and away
from the death of that long summer:

black men murdered by fear
and rage, bombs in airports, the forty-nine

in my hometown who'd never again
catch their own eyes

in a dance club mirror and wonder
what the night ahead

might bring, even that TV madman grabbing
for power, all of it

gave way to the moon
on the wind-threshed water—the light shattered

and therefore multiplied.
                                        Now, looking back

from this aftermath, what does it mean
to know such a moment

is over, to try and accept it will not return—
at least not as it was, at least not

for us? That night, we surrendered
to radiance, drank in as much good light

as we could. Can any of that flickering still live
inside us? And, if it does, how must we break

open to let it shine again?
                                        Now, when

that day, remembered, is a mausoleum
with all the lights left on—a fiery reminder

that every day of every year
that follows will hold a little less

brightness, darkness steadily reclaiming
ground—can we ever again avert our eyes,

for even an instant, from history
to give ourselves to beauty?

Perhaps we shouldn't; but I want to.

Miguel M. Morales

ELDERS

HIM

They have all three branches now.

What are they going to take from us?

What can they take from us?

There's nothing left.

We fought and protested Reagan and Bush

in the 80s and 90s for what little we have.

We're old and alone.

We're supposed to be enjoying life now.

We're too old to go back out

on the streets and protest.

ME

No. Young people need us to show them
how we survived those years.
Just like those elders showed us
            during the AIDS crisis.
They taught us how to turn our rage and anger
into tools and into action in order to save lives
            and save ourselves.
Maybe we are too old to go back out
on the streets and protest but
they need us and we need them.

We are the elders now.

Eloisa Amezcua

ELEGY
Nov. 9, 2016

I woke up wanting
to have children

less than I wanted
them when I went

to bed. I can't
imagine why I'd

be so careless.
I look out the window

& see my neighbor
drive past in her car

laughing perhaps
at the radio, her

pale hand reaching
for the dial. & for

a moment, I'm
envious of the way

the light turns
her blonde hair

translucent, how
in the backseat

her baby sleeps
unscathed. I want

to laugh till
my womb falls out

between my legs—
a bloody Rorschach

splatter— & there
is no more wanting.

I know now
how this world

can turn a body
into an urn.

Philip Matthews

ELECTION DAY

—Then again, there is the squabbling,
leashed meat in Aisle 6, roaring its bloody,
soft gums. How it does prowl
in its Styrofoam tray. How it does sleep in the light.
Before the hands swept in, before even the employees,
I was here, having slept on the floor, pouring prayers
to the cutlets and priest-joints. How it does protect itself
against the primacy of money. I am swaying my arms.
I am praising and praising and praising
as the carts roll by my martyr. How it does sniff at the herbs
in its former life it ate for itself. How it does shine
through its cover, wet ruby.

Derek Coyle

READING JOHN ASHBERY
IN COSTA COFFEE, CARLOW

I am thirsty, and want more than a mocha,
iced, mint, or otherwise, can provide.
James Joyce is in the corner,
I recognise the white cane, dark glasses.
Indeed, it is him, having an auld chat
with Patrick Kavanagh, weighing up the various
merits and de-merits of the Kerr's Pink potato. Joyce
misses the cafes of Paris,
but the virtues of a solid Kerr's Pink
are some form of consolation.
My phone rings and it's John Lennon,
asking, "Who shot J.R.?" It's for a table quiz
they are hosting in the afterlife,
having grown bored of croquet
on their rather too perfect, eternally summer, lawns.
Roy Orbison and Genghis Khan
are on the table that's leading
at the minute, with Lennon's team
a close second. Lennon is pretty certain
Gandhi has cheated on a few questions.
He's on table three.

In many ways it is the centre of the world.
It's hectic on a Sunday before Christmas
and you never know who will wander in.
It was the Pizza Hut, but that never
took off for reasons nobody
has ever really explained to me.
Mecca, Lourdes, or even Las Vegas
have nothing on it. If it wasn't too cold
we'd even have a naked cowboy
on the Hanover Roundabout, only
he'd be playing a big silver banjo
instead of a guitar.

There's a guy over in the corner
I fancy from the gym. He's shit hot.
I'm pretty sure his walk is not 100% straight.

When this place was the Pizza Hut
I had my Sunday lunch here
with my lover, whom I was really mad about.
He liked it, over the Indian
down the road I brought him to
the week before. I think it was a competition thing.
I told him I thought it was a bit
packaged, you know, it's not quite organic.
There's a woman over there
with bright pink hair. I think
it clashes somewhat with her red dress.
I meet my friends Simon and Rozz here sometimes.
They are good fun.
They introduced me to the porridge.
There's a man comes in here regular.
He's got a beard, doesn't work,
but looks well in his leather jacket and jeans.
I think he's a member of the I.R.A.

There's a continuous flow of people
at the counter. Right now,
I think they are all very dull,
all blue jeans, grey coats and tops.
I know it's wintertime,
but that doesn't mean you can't wear summer
all year around.
That man who's just emerged from the jacks
is a theologian (I know by his jacket),
he's just ignored the woman behind him,
failing to hold the door ajar for her.
She's a saint, ironically enough,
I can tell by the blue nimbus
hanging around her head. No fan
will ever blow it away.

You'd never think there was a major crisis
in world politics. Children are being blown-up in Syria.
In London right now, bombings being planned.
There's a man I saw in the mirror in the jacks,
he thinks the Four Horsemen of the Apocalypse
are just about to appear in the sky
over Woodie's. He's pretty convinced
Genghis Khan will be riding one of them,
with John Lennon on another, a dynamo
on the crossbow, having had loads
of time to practice, and he's bored.
Shooting minnows can be great fun.

Oswaldo Vargas

SANCTUARY MOVEMENT 2.0

When Trump
comes for me

will you be down
for me?

Will you be

moving floorboards
for me

sweet-talking agents
for me

fund my passage back
for me

be the water jug at the border
for me

Sanctuary Movement 2.0
for me?

Anthony Lioi

CHOIRPUNK

John Coltrane sounded in a dream,
surrounded by seraphic flame—
with a face like unto jazz itself.

He said:

Don't worry, man,
the answers to this test
count.

First question: A choir hears:
a. all creatures as a riff on God's breath
b. a million voices crying out, then silence—
c. the Force that rolled away the rock

(What is this Jedi shit? I said)

Shut
the eff
up.

Third answer:

Punk: a quire of trouble
American idiot's bad breath
a poisoned boy band
a kick in the balls for all the right reasons
a Pussy Riot prison break

a vavasour of funk.

Last Sunday, Father Whatawaste had a thought

on the Trinity

lasting twenty minutes, an eternity

Altar punks snore

and show their fillings.

Extra credit question: Be there

altar punks in heaven?

Hey Spicer, here's unversion for you,
Jack Kerouac: a fifth of the dharma,
Di di Prima sez it's wicked good:

I call Dead Kennedys to bless this book
Summon neighbor dogs to croon this hook
May Johnny Kepler chant elliptic harmony
for those vicious kids, Sid and Nancy
so I sound like less of a schnook!

Next question, Coltrane sez:

Of a sudden you're super,
whose bubble would you burst?
Who would you target first:
Monsanto? BP? Some unspecified other?
Why will everything that dies

call you brother?

O Cyndi Lauper,

Siouxsie Sioux

O Betty Davis

We cry unto you

help us aspire—a Nasty Music

for the punk that is to come!

Till then, Giordano Bru', *don't cave, baby, to the lies*

Till then, Joanie d'Arc, *keep Angles close, but bishops closer,*

Till then, my Enemy, *don't believe the hype*

Though the choir's sad to say it—

Kauser Ahmed

—a nice girl from Paramus—once conveyed it:

Certain persons don't deserve to be obeyed.

Karen Hayes

MARGINALIZED

See this person
respect this person
love this person

you don't get to pick
you don't get to choose

which one
or only some

love

is more pliable
than we think

do it

even if it's hard
even if you disagree

even if the person

doesn't see
won't respect
can't love
you

Andi Boyd

MY COUNTRY IS A HAND

It comes as knuckle first, that tastes like root
ginger root, maybe, sugar cane, the tongue flips
backwards to taste, instead, the knuckle grows a bone,
a fist, a long arm that suffocates from inside, squashes
the mouth until teeth fall out. It arrives large as a bed,
around the body
is warm

is crawling the skin like spider legs, many-fingered,
which tickle, which make one laugh like a child,
and then swell the skin, turn it raw and red if one could see
red or any other color for it grows and blocks the sky
falls atop
is caging

grappling against, then pulling it to kiss the palm,
which slaps against the jaw, holds the hip too long
which smells like your mother, which is corn eaten,
which is required to hold a spoon to the mouth.

which is used to flick a trigger

a hand that is my country

a hand that is what my country has decided for me.

Liz Lampman

BETTER ARMOR

I.

Are we through yet,
    mother? Our speaking
        lilts, trills as a loon
call burning the surface
    of wide water with
        silent, blue flame.
It yowls as a stray
    cat's guttural resistance
        against me, my sweater
wrapped around her matted
    fur and bones. When
        were our last gentle
words? You say
    you never filled me—
        I wouldn't latch, or
there wasn't enough
    milk—we'll never know.
        Have those months
of hunger really lingered
    until now? So long
        that my body joins
yours under gravity's thumb.

II.

Parable of the wanton
    daughter: born with dark
        tufts of willfulness shading
her eyes. Prone to high living,
    the old laws wouldn't
        stick. She ate the premature
fruit, taut and chalky.

Sought another willing child
        and they lapped the strange
and nameless flavors of their skin.
    With the taste of flesh
        on her pink tongue,
she left the crèche
    for libertine affairs
        —fell for the crackle
and spark down spine
    to whip. Then followed a row
        of bodies to the coast
as a student of touch. Later,
    wiser and almost sated,
        she returned home
a teacher with embodied
    pedagogy and a corporeal text.

III.

You know, mother.
    I am slut;
        I am she. You act
as if the thought of sex
    destroys you, but it's a funny,
        lovely thing when done
right. Would you leave me
    with a raked world,
        her crotch tattered from
grab-hands, and implore me
    to look away from her
        bleeding in the corner? Listen,
we are all endangered,
    but we can't go back
        to the breast. Its milk
acrid to grown tongues.
    It is taking back that will
        save us—the body,
my temple, not God's.

Cut the weft of caution,
it's a banner of fear—
just look at safety, stolen
all over. No matter how precious
the mother finds the child,
she cannot stay the levy
when the water rises.
One more rape
and the last glacier is sure
to flush the land. Enough
of this vendetta.
Let me tell you my story
and melt down words
like *purity* into better armor.
We may need to sink in
our claws to let
the world's bad blood.
I need the first body
I touched with my mouth
by my side. Mother,
other daughters need us,
our cries like sirens'
will wreck the ships of bad men.

Guy Traiber

ALL THE SQUARES TURNED TO HOUSES

In the night the square filled with crowds
of men and silence. All the squares
have turned to houses of prayer and gossips
and bad word and winds. A wind of change
and an eastern wind and other spirits.
In the night the truth is naked
that is why the people are all hidden.
In the night we stopped being
hands and blooming hearts, we stopped
lying in the language of love;
love thy neighbour as thyself, *Homo homini*
lupus, these are all the teachings while standing
on one foot. On two feet the number of teachings multiplies
further, like the number of squares and ivory towers.
Before dawn the moon stood bright and mighty in the coldness
and we woke up and loved each other with naked bodies
devoid of lies. Our eyes faced
the loneliness of the world.

Mitchell King

WHEN DOES CAPTAIN AMERICA ARRIVE?

I have placed all my hopes with men in skin tight tights deflecting
lasers and side eye, ignoring *who is this bitch?* by brandishing the truth
as a shield and a weapon of life against insurgent

death—in the country where I come from everyone knows hate—
hate at a theatre, hate at a night club, hate at a mall;
can his bicep lift the weight of our pain?

I wait by the mirror and hold my head down—is this shame?
Hating others as I have hated myself, escaping to midnight fantasies—
wearing a latex cape and hood, saving the world with words

at night and walking, quietly, to work by day. His shield must be
like Achilles' covered in faces long dead and still fighting, circling
a perimeter of magic metal, avenging steel, bas-relief, a carved history
of war and the struggle against. I check

my watch watching the arc of the sun against sundial—it is damn
near dark—the wolves are paw-pacing beyond this base camp I have made
from news-scraps and artillery shells in a school long dead.
I want to throw down the walls of every city

that forbid us entry, or I want to colonize the moon, riding Cap's shield
like a rocket thrown out into the unclaimed space between stars by a bicep
that is a locomotive agent for *Freedom*!, Wranglers and change like

a poem stronger than myself—that can stand on stanzas like sturdy legs
and redeem others as I have wanted to be redeemed in a place between
death and Elysium: America, as she could be, star-fagged and star-spangled,
where a hero might not be needed—

but here all the words I know are dead.

Kai Coggin

VIBRATION

My words
have been dormant
in this post-election storm,
lying in wait
while hate
is made the new norm,
lying like soft bullets all around me,
scattered, disjoined, unformed,
the word TOLERANCE
is hiding behind the dresser,
the word HOPE
is lying quiet
atop a laundry heap on the floor,
the word PEACE
is trapped at the bottom of a bottle,
the word LOVE
is the sound of a closing door.

My words,
soft
bullets
that will never bruise,
that will never pierce through skin,
that will never call for blood,
these words
and so many others
wait like an artillery of dreams
in the moonlit minefield of my consciousness,
waiting for exposure,
waiting for me to take a step
into the unknown territory of this jilted demo(n)cracy,
and use my voice even more for
what is good,
what is light,
what is freedom,
what is fight.

The haze is wearing off,
the smoke of disbelief,
the shock of godlessness,
a renewal of promise
made into the still-star-filled sky,
that my voice
is a weapon of beauty,
my pen is a sword of truth,
my hands trembling across the keys will not fail us.
WORDS, come back to me,
let's fight together in this revolution,
I am gathering you up,
soft bullets,
forming you into explosions of light,
into rockets' glare of blue paradigms,
into penetrating booms of grace,
into a 21-heart salute
of what can I do to make the world better today?

This is not some hippy delusion;
it is the means
by which to survive these next four years.
For me, it is gathering together WORDS
and forming them
into precise vibrations of outrage and hope,
it is illuminating every act
of conscious movement toward good,
it is knowing privilege
and using it to amplify marginalized voices,
it is vigilance against all forms of hate,
it is exposing darkness
with bright magnifications of truth,
it is combating fear
with a promise to band together and fight,
it is building bridges wherever they try to build a wall,
it is protecting each other,
it is protecting our stories,
protecting our rights,
protecting our dignity,
protecting our humanity.

This is the new old america,
the united divided states,
the blood red states and borders,
the blue lighthouses of tomorrow,
our fears are continually justified,
this is a real human ache,
his rancorous rhetoric is rippling out to the masses,
the rotten stench of long-silenced hate
is coming up through the floorboards of our country,
but this is NOT our collective fate.

At least now we know the hate is still there,
we know exactly where to find it,
we can see the white robes in the light of day.

Still,
there are
MORE OF US on the side of inclusion,
MORE OF US on the side of love,
MORE OF US on the side of oneness,
MORE OF US on the side of equality,
MORE OF US on side of healing the environment,
MORE OF US on the side of resistance to hatred,
MORE OF US on the side of freedom from tyranny,
MORE OF US on the side of light and beauty
there are MORE OF US
and we will not be silent,
and we will not bend,
and we will not stop our trajectory of spiritual evolution,
this is a mountain,
but we are ready for the climb,
we have already tasted the clouds.

Sometimes a catalyst for real and lasting change
comes in the most difficult circumstance,
sometimes it takes a rampant wildfire
to rebuild a broken house,
so today,
I renew my purpose as a poet,
I am coming out of my quiet disillusion,

I am gathering up my words
and taking a step into this dark unknown,

aiming poems

forged out of invisibility and fire,
ready to light everything I possibly can
with a vibration of hope.

torrin a. greathouse

THE CALLOUSES TO SHOW FOR IT

for M.

it is a week after the election, after the fires have husked this city &
spread & LA is rumbling like the ghosts of unbuilt freeways
announcing their names & we are still grasping at blades
of grass, burnt copper straw in the sun, surprised when we pull

our palms away bloody. my lover lays their head against my chest &
tells me *i am searching for the pattern in the unevenness of your heartbeat*
& by this they mean: it is so hard to tell from a shattered mirror where
it first began breaking & i tell them *callouses form wherever the skin*

is scraped away, maybe the rough topography of my pulse is only
the natural response to pressure & by this i mean: i have never texted
the words "home" & "safe" so much, i wish i had the callouses to show
for it & they say *i can see your pulse in your neck, it's so strange* & by this

they mean: how strange to see your blood still within you, drumbeat
against tight skin & not fear it's draining & to not whisper safety in
to pillows like confession. i kiss them, help them dress. borrowed boxers,
binder neatly rolled, pull them close, feel their heart's unsteady pounding.

i say nothing & by this i mean: i'm on my way darling i will be home safe soon.

Ray Sharp

OH AMERICA

Oh, America, you big stupid brute, I love
your huevos rancheros and black coffee,
the way you dance on Saturday night,
your Southern accent and blue denim,
soft magnolia breeze and white-washed
clapboard church. You are my neighbor,
my old girlfriend, my demented uncle
who makes me turn away in shame from
such crazy talk, so much blood spilled,
wiped on your shirt. Isn't it about time
you grew up and opened your heart to love?

Jacob Budenz

IN PROTEST
OF THE FIRST AMENDMENT DEFENSE ACT

A droplet on a petal—
dirty water, wet daisy,
my hand slid into yours
and you bit the flesh of my
chest softly, tasting.

A hot coal on a cold heart—
sweat dripped from fingertips,
splashed on my eager tongue,
and you plucked the hairs from my
scalp slowly, taking.

A quick dive into the sea—
tan skin and tiny splash,
I waded, waiting, drowned in doubt
as you held down my thick
head smoothly, treading.

A promise, a souvenir—
two black suits on a white
cake, pieces taken, one by one,
you placed the foam on waiting
plates sweetly, trembling.

Bob Carr

CENSOR APPROACHING

On my tongue   font size
letters   measured by a ruler

the thrown switch of the state
approaching   silence

Drugged by a phone
flag-gagged   on the news-reel

tight   threads of fish line
tourniquet   my dry pen

Speaking volumes   in 140 character
fragments   the censor's tweets

sparse   My left hand curly
over   erasure

pinkie skin unstained
Tied   strapped   I scribble

Out of laminate black   the desktop grows
a wired chair   rocks

Laura Rena Murray

DIVIDED

if our civil rights movement
lost leaders
to murder
and still persisted
how do we maintain that momentum?
instead of reverting
to the defensive
position

if ICWA and welfare
were meant to serve as reparations
we still do not understand
the depth of the damage
our ancestors wrought
measured by blood quantum
and a poverty line

how much
is the percentage
of your impoverishment?

how little can we give?

for food so you do not starve
enough to afford
carbs
that leave you empty
and give you diabetes

for rental assistance
worthless vouchers become
dangled carrots
while cramming you into mass-
assembled beds
in shelters
and in prison

and always

into churches
where you are advised
strongly
to kneel and pray
for redemption
for salvation
for deliverance
from this world

there is something
wrong
about a world
divided
by those who are
white
to maintain
distance
from everyone
else.

Breana Steele

SAFETY PIN

When I cannot bring myself
to fasten a safety pin to my sweater
this November, I get a small taste of fearing
visibility, of fearing for your life
because people see you,
and I realize whiteness has protected me
more than I'd known even while acknowledging
privilege. Because a safety pin can be taken
off, for my own safety. Blackness—
that can't be removed.

I can become invisible. I can become one of them.

Sure, I walk to my car at night with keys
between fingers. Sure, when I get in,
I whip my head around to check
the backseat for attackers. Sure, nights
are dreams of being killed,
raped, always, always
by men.

They never have faces I remember, but this man,
this man who has taken it all, taken the highest
office,

he could be one of them.

RE Katz

A CONTROLLED FALL

Your foot touches the floor thirty times and your foot touches the thirty four times each and with each step you think of a name thirty times a name thirty names for love/for same love/for the same love you won good/for the good riot of touching the floor of pouring one out of pooring out of poor poor out out out/get out poor to get alive out/get out of of the house if you come out now/get out.

Do porn or get out alive/do porn to get out alive/do a lively porn to come out/come out alive/come out now/come out national/national come out of poor day.

Say the name that is your own/say the shuffle tap fall forward in a controlled way/fall forward when you tap your feet/fall because you dance fall because you have no balance/fall because your balance was lost/OKAY stolen last fall/taken/you were pushed to the ground/fall for that/fall for anything but get out alive/get out/poor getout you live falling down.

Your foot touches the ground and you are already dead/thirty times dead/ dead at thirty/get out thirty poor times you falling down pushed/you pushed/you had to push/you pushed and pushed and pushed/call if getting out/pushed alive/a controlled fall/when they're on you/call.

The fallen fall from a dead height/we mourn and move/we move to mourn the dead dance darkening drum of sweat dew/someone's breath on your neck/fall on you/you poor getout/you fell'd go-getter/get gone before/ murderbox we watch you on/say

WHEN I AM GONE I AM DEAD WITH JOY.

When we say your name we say/we are willing to get out alive for you/we fouled to save you/we failed you/we fucking failed you.

Jim Elledge

THAT ONE OVER

That one over
there who's
huddled
against the darkness
on the far side
of the camp fire,
that guy's skinny
as a splinter
of pine straw
and dies
every night, night
after night *if*
you take
his screaming
seriously.

A.A.

REBELLION

Won't you celebrate me:
left my country at 12,
lost my identity at 13,
discovered I couldn't return at 14,
contemplated suicide at 16 and 17
and on certain occasions, like
last Tuesday. I found myself
at the knees of poetry
and every word that has tried
to kill me grows as a new layer
of black skin.

Seth Pennington

FENCE

The yard was dry grass and dust,
the printed path of dogs running their territory,
yelling down even the quiet steps
of neighbors. Stones covered
holes where bones were buried then dug then eaten then
shit. The fence was erupting. Nails
pushed out of wood, jutting tongues and spears. Whole
sections leaned far enough to break. The dogs barked
at the splinter. Men came with screws, cement,
a fresh wall. The dogs peeled their faces past smiles.
What they were became teeth: chewing,
pacing; they ate at shovel blades and boot heels.
If a man sat, they bit into his ears. He went
bleeding to building the wall. The dogs crowed
some kind of laughter into the wet
waiting for the Quikrete to set. The men packed
back into their trucks with their worn boots and their
check. The dogs screamed the men off into
the headlight of nightfall. Dust fogged over
the land with the dirt getting clawed into maps
and the maps falling apart. Neighbors
walked quiet and quick, heads bent, ducking
the backyard baritones until the dogs fell asleep
in their satisfaction, across the cool of their stones,
what was buried under the muscle of them.

Nicole Connolly

CRYBABY

I tell my mom that, as a queer woman,
Donald Trump's looming administration makes me

feel unsafe; she tells me, *you won't always*
get what you want, words recycled from

television men: They call me a whiner, ruined
by a participation-ribbon-flooded childhood

staining me green, but the president-elect loves
his participation ribbon, the pride flag he held

upside-down when he said at least he'll keep
Muslims from killing us—pitting the oppressed

against each other like stray dogs with cages of teeth
for hearts, and when I ask my part-Palestinian friend,

are you safe?, he says his community is behind
him—though, the next day, a man there forces

a woman to take off her hijab under threat
of being set on fire, lighter to head. Why

shouldn't I cry to kill this flame? Especially
when I cannot think of anyone more in love

with participation ribbons than the church
of my parents. I saw the basket of baby bottles

stationed outside their steeple, nipples off, mouths
gaping for Washingtons, trophies for mothers

who kept babies they didn't want. How can
it still surprise me? These people who do

anything to ensure you participate in even
one moment of life, no matter what else

happens to you once you get here.

Francine Hendrickson

SEE THE ENTIRE COUNTRY BEFORE YOU DIE

Neon red Amerikkka. Underbelly Amerikkka. Deep fried Oreo Amerikkka. Country of ice cube sweating in a diner. Country of privilege and husked corn. Amerikkka of cis men who don't like my shorts and piss on my car. Amerikkka where we dress our fear in black. Amerikkka where fear is a cancer. Amerikka where I can breathe in the company of so few people without being "she." Amerikkka who calls on the President Vice to electro shock the queer out of me. *We just want to be free, of you* said Amerikkka. Dance club is church in Amerikkka. *Your church is a festering blister* said Amerikkka. Explain Pulse to my kids Amerikkka. Keep pulse in my friends Amerikkka. *You chose your death* said Amerikkka. My Amerikkkan foot sliced open in a river so cold I feel nothing. Amerikkka starving the Amerikkka out of Amerikkkans to stay fed in Amerikkka. I starve out my own fear to stay alive in Amerikkka. I can't feel my own fingers in Amerikkka. I can't feel my face Amerikkka. *We erased the name of your love* said Amerikkka. *You are wounded, unwanted, and showing* said Amerikkka. *Disassociate harder* said Amerikkka. *Disassociate harder* said Amerikkka. Drive to the body of water I was born by. Miles of land unfolds. *You are not mine* said Amerikkka. Does salt water not rise to itself?

Michael G. Federspiel

HERE

Here: the "I" does not exist and it does not echo.
The eye throbs with the muscles
the ear is too tired to move.
An ear: drum without a mallet
covered in a flesh-tarp.
There: caverns are different
not rocky or pointed
but malleable.
An eye: a pause-in-the-VHS-tape.
Blink.
Blink.
To be: is not to be. To exist.
To hear: is not to hear To see.
To see: is not just to see. To hear.

Gentle reminders
every few seconds:
To spell is to cut the air.
To do is to hold a cup of tea.
to weave a basket.
To look is to hold a sea to your eyes
moving your head clockwise
jostled in a paper boat
or longing to hear hesitations in the moon
Some say that our ribs vibrate
identical frequencies
with the universe
attuned to the planets' waltz
This is how we dance
Although, I wouldn't say
that your dance
or mine
are any more human.
Gender is divided
along the bridge of the nose

where a flag has been uprooted.
where we have dug my interstice.

A philtrum canyon
assembling a steeper cliff from fingers
just to call you ugly.
Wiping tears takes a forked graze
along the apple of the cheek.
Wine.
Family is two wolves standing side-by-side
Each with one paw mangled—but touching.
Their heads outlined
beneath a canopy of trees.

Grotesque are those who hear
the song of our lifted bodies
across the floor
and ask us to come apart
yet still we cleave to the spool
as we unravel
Help:

is the ocean catching a rock
by the elbow
i n the white of a wave's head.

"I" stands at the divide between
the heart
and the seams of interlaced fingers
floating at the chasm between languages:
at the site of choice.

Choice: a rooted "V"
held together by bones and sapling limbs
can also mean the two of us
together.

A dream is a red sniper's dot

in the middle of the forehead
removed like a child's sticker.

(K)not nearly severs the jugular
slicing its way through the lower jaw
joint of wrist counter-clockwise from the trachea.
Bad is to clap one's hands,
excitement at a meeting of the flesh without sound.
Good is to invert the world.
To praise is to tremble,
to acknowledge a dark opening,
an ellipse with the eyes
finding center at origin,
an eclipse box
pinhole projector,
as if hope lies in wait.

Lachan Brown

AMERICARNAGE

after artwork by Tony Curran titled:
Nothing's syncing to the cloud from the offices of NPR

The angled timestamp shows my
stunned face under the map of red
states, constantly hitting f5 instead
of breathing. There are dangers close by,

and the small screen can't distractify
us anymore, because the dragon's head
rises from its electoral chamber, shred-
ding all November predictions. If I

turn my gaze I can see a full glass
overflowing, so someone will need to
make those pollsters g(y)rate again.

But for now, may the first be last,
or another loser come into view,
beneath the demagogue's shitty refrain.

Jacob Lotter

LOVE SONG FOR A GAY BOY

On my way to loving you I learned
that love sucks like you do and
heartbreak is not just a metaphor, it turns

because suck has multiple meanings. Burn
this page and suck it up because
on my way to loving you I learned

that blow jobs don't suck, and are earned
when you're not flamboyant and admit
heartbreak is not just a metaphor, it turns

into meetings with boys that happen once and adjourn
after they cum too quickly and you remember
that on my way to loving you I learned

to man up, suck less, act less forlorn—more forlorn.
Does sadness make you tougher or does it remind you that
heartbreak is not just a metaphor, it turns

into hiding pain and lies and truths
and not loving a man that loves you, meaning that
on my way to loving you I learned
that heartbreak is not just a metaphor, it turns.

Clare Paniccia

LETTER BEGINNING WITH TWO LINES BY DONALD TRUMP

after Matthew Olzmann

You could see there was blood coming out of her eyes, blood
coming out of her wherever as if it was wrong to know the

blood of the fledgling woman present in my thigh's
crease, the bird that had come down and out of me

as a shocked and muddied thing. I was sure that all girls
had them—their colonies: nests of swallows crowding

under lung or in the base of the spine, birds that burst
forth a rapid sweetness of new sex, the just-birthed, the pink

roe of us a blush of ribbon or fresh-bloomed bouquet.
No one had told me that inside was a field of fertile ground,

that our wombs were opening and we were standing on
the precipice of change—that to imagine a new star or galaxy

in its spinning was only a portion of our becoming, as if
our bodies had been held and shifted toward the slightest

angle, this juncture of form, our uniform skirts as accidental
flags of crimson, our hands cupping our tenderness. Tell me,

isn't it beautiful, the way our bodies root into earth to draw
out strength—the way they command their fluid. That if I held

onto a girl's arm I would feel the grip of our ancestor's
turning, the carbon and atom that congregated on a chalice

of bone to make her, her frame—that if I looked up past
her cheek I would see a nova's burn concealed in the crux of

her eye. The wing of a passerine dipping out from the corner
of its perch.

Brian Czyzyk

THE BLAME GAME

She says *any woman who can't handle her husband shouldn't*
handle nuclear codes as if she could erase the trail of spit
slicked across her best friend's belly by her boyfriend's tongue
by yanking her own long hair out of its ponytail, or wearing
crimson lipstick so his eyes would stick there, on her mouth.
Or she could love him more. Bring him a bowl of Doritos
every half hour during the Super Bowl. Then he'd never leave.

As if a wife is solely responsible for her husband's wandering
eye. As if that same shade of lipstick was meant for one man
and could never be smeared by another's knuckles. When she's shoved
down in shadow and feels her underwear slide, she imagines
her boyfriend's dark hair pooling atop her friend's knees—her moans
the countdown—his hand approaching the launch button between her thighs.

Collin Kelley

FROM THE AIR

this continent is a jigsaw puzzle,
full of shapes and patterns—
perfect squares of farmland
and alien crop circles.

And from space
the cities are cathedrals of light—
points of navigations to guide us
when the road is hidden in darkness.

Up here, no one questions
your patriotism, your beliefs,
who you have chosen to love—
those are earthbound concerns.

Get up, off the ground, take wing
or you'll never see the whole—
the patchwork nation we truly are
held together by invisible string.

A quilt is only as sturdy as the fabric
and the seamster's precise fingers—
the needle pulled high and taut
before plunging back into layers.

Don't be afraid to prick your finger
and always prick up your ears
when others try to define your freedom.
My darlings, there will always be blood.

Ysabel Y. Gonzalez

MY MOTHER'S HOUSE

The blade still has green on its tip
from swinging at bamboo, machete
hanging over our warm fireplace like
Basquiat art in a museum.

I've stared too long and plan
to free it from the house's wall.
It belongs inside a firm grip, slicing
upward, creating red paths before a daughter.

Did my mother hold it with cracked
nails digging deep into a palm?
I've heard so many long stories
which found their way to this quick ending

and I start at the beginning again
until I recall how to lift a weapon
again, because I am my mother again
and I am my mother's mother again

and so the memory goes like smoke
dancing on fingertips, lifting them
from slumber. Wake, you weapons
crafted to cope, designed to trim the dead

from around the land's gash, steel
birthed from brown women's hands
to protect this house, my mother's house—
my house. Land which gives everyone a pass

except to the women that harvest
this black, black earth. Oh!
My house, my machete, my reaped
America, how short our memory is.

In the long stories my mother tells,
America belonged once to no one.
It has always been borrowed. But
we fight for this much again and again and

the loop searches, finds us in
my mother's house again
with a sleeping machete, a waking machete
again, and I start at the beginning

again, until I can recall
until I lift a weapon again,
in my mother's house
again, in my house, again,

Freesia McKee

UNRAVELING THE TARGET

The motor on my fan sounds
like a rattle. I pick up the same
book I always pick up because

the poems are short. Today it is raining
a lot. One sharp burst of thunder.
The motor on my fan will take

my fan apart. The screws and glue
slowly loosening. We drive and eat

something called fairy food, hard
and crunchy. We cry in the car
on the way home. The machine of something

can take that thing apart. The whirring
and regular job can be the thing's demise.
I learned to love

unequivocally and without hold. It's hard
to say with this rainstorm up. I mean being in pain.
A problem of machinery.

Robert Auld

ADHESION

I don't get out of bed the day
before the election in America,

but dream of walking down a street
toward my old elementary school

where the curtain of the polling booth
draws itself behind me. I draw

a future for myself with a sleight
of hand, fingernails painted blue

for the occasion, to make a flag
of myself, fag with guilty conscience,

future of termination either
way. Binary. Beaten out.

The beating of eggs cracked
on the side of the counter,

making breakfast with my lover
the morning of November 8th 2016.

I often forget the eggs were
once alive, fork the yolk

to blur the image. I vote
from a similar blind side.

The blue nail polish briefly catches
the fluorescent light in the gymnasium.

The shimmer is delicious.
In its glare, I fill the box.

Charlie Bondhus

an excerpt from "PROCESSING"

Facebook's filled with articles   & insight

spray paint on the very concrete   [[[[[wall of bathroom

community college

deserved it   is where white

unrelated to drumpf & apropos of nothing but my own survival

I was   in an intake ward   last year at this time

& white walls became   leitmotif for

in the ensuing year   which is now and now

it's my fault this is a   r a c i s t s e x i s t x e n o p h o

to grieve   my own abuse while chastising

absorption to right measure   when my white, man-

even while

up   while brown people   killed from neck

abstract   populism   &   disenfranchisement

Satanic mills" & warehouses & weigh stations

my Clonazepam tastes like government

re: abstract fear & anxiety & grieving &

stall at

where build the wall is where last year *Mike Brown*

liberals couldn't happen here is me & anxiety

did you know

where the blue light (bluer than the scrubs)

MAAADDDDNNNEEESSSS

there's guilt for grieving though more for not grieving

a n s p h o b i c i s l a m o p h o b i c country but I'm trying

self-

shaped body shields me

it kills from neck

down & up & this is all concrete

as absolution closure of the "dark

job privilege I need & rail against

H.B.K.

THE SABBATH

It was the Sabbath after the world ended quietly
to a backdrop of screaming
and I went to a Bet Midrash
to stop working
on being
and reflect
on breathing
And there they shared a story about burning palaces
and the men who try
to put out those fires
And I thought this was important not because
men set the world on fire
but because
we did
and those men are trying
to put us out
And I thought about my moral need
to not let people burn
when their own palaces
are on fire
And I thought about
walking down a street
to the sound of popping embers
and not seeing
the sign in the front yard
telling me that
this is a controlled burn
a cleansing flame
intentional
And I thought about calling the police
if I trusted them
enough
to save the people in that palace
or if I trusted myself enough
to do it instead

And I thought about
the palaces I would like to burn
and the people who still
live in those castles
the people who might call for help
not knowing that the fire
is supposed to
save us

Savannah Sipple

WHEN THOSE WHO HAVE THE POWER START TO LOSE IT, THEY PANIC

They rut young girls.   They come   to play. They carry their wallets in front pockets, checkbooks
in glove boxes.   Money. No money.   They drink beer.   They drink bourbon.
                    [She shouldn't have been drinking.]   They say shit like
boys will be boys   and   *you have to consider his side of the story*   they mean his side of the story
is the only one that matters   *there's two sides*   Girls should live legs open and mouths shut.
Go to church and dress up.
                    [What was she wearing?]
They four-wheel on weekends.   They ride in golf carts,   in ubers,   on bicycles. They get
elected President. They want their girls tough enough to ride shotgun, limber enough to stretch
across backseats,   across laps,   against doors,   in back alleys,
behind dumpsters
                    [She was out too late].   They want girls
sober enough to see,   drunk enough to see double,   *two sides!*   to moan,
no sounds like yes to their ears. No sounds like yes to their ears.   *Don't tell me no*.
                    [She had a mouth on her]   unless
we're talking about how twenty minutes might ruin the rest of their lives, then *No!—*
wait—we don't deserve this. *There are two sides!*   *Listen to me!*
They don't fuck up,   do they?   They get up, pay 25 million dollars, walk away.
                    [She shouldn't have even been there.]

Ed Madden

SECURITY

"I will say that people who are following me are very passionate. They love this country and they want this country to be great again." – Donald Trump, 19 Aug 2015, after learning that two supporters beat and urinated on a homeless Latino man

Today is thick mist, as if the clouds were too heavy, resting
against the earth, giving up. The end of the street is mist;

we can't know what's there, though we know the septic creek, security
cameras that point both ways, the blind corner, the house where the hoarder

once lived, all dog urine, food wrappers, Happy Meal toys still packed
in cellophane, bought up cheap by a man who cleaned it all out,

then cut down all the trees, fifty years of growth and blossoms, gone—

the house saved, the yard razed. A neighbor tells us there are drug deals
at a house down the street, the old man there getting street meds

for his pain, he's dying. We didn't know. We shake our heads; these things
can't be fixed. We won't know evil when it comes. We will call it

something else, something we love. It will look like something we love.

Our families, our neighbors will shake their heads at our unreasonable sadness.
A cousin posts a picture of a white girl in a patriotic hat, crying—

their image of the resistance: silly, misled, wrong. We won't know evil
when it comes, we won't. It will look like something or someone we love.

It will point its finger elsewhere: *that*, it will say, is evil, those people,
those people, and those.

Isaiah Vianese

PIGEON

keeps working.
He preps for wind,
the peril of living
five flights up.
He fortifies his roost
with feather, grass,
bits of plastic & wrapper.

Sometimes, rain
floods his work
or cold forces the bird
to other havens,
but he always emerges
to mend what is broken,
to love what was not lost.

Jeremy Brunger

GAY SEX KILLS FASCISM

I grew eight horizontal inches when the fascists
barebacked Tennessee. Gay sex kills fascism.
Oh, lovely, half-living—want to stroke
this machine? I do not sing, for my throat
is full of fluttering angels I drowned,
or, rather, that were drowned in me.
No good man has good luck. Only fuck.
Gay sex kills fascism entirely. We say
people may know of truth, are valuable
in themselves and represent a humanism.
To die—I reply, gritting these teeth: no,
we do not heavenly glow. We only think so.

Liz Ahl

OTHERS CARRIED MILK

"Within the crowd at least one person was wearing goggles and carrying a stick, others carried milk—a tactic known to be used to decontaminate pepper spray, and medics were on hand." – Burlington, VT Police Department press release, offered to characterize a nonviolent crowd of protesters as violent in order to justify the police department's violent response

"Hope is never silent." – Harvey Milk

Others carried signs, a tactic known to enable free speech, written messages, dangerously sharp puns and slogans.

Others carried pocketbooks, a tactic known to keep sunglasses and spare change from spilling its deadly shrapnel out onto the pavement.

Others carried fists full of air.

Others carried pocket copies of the Constitution, a tactic known to be used for creating the U.S. government and enshrining fundamental rights, the sharp corners of which have been known to be used for putting out an eye.

Others carried cell phones, a tactic known to enable talking to other people on other cell phones.

Others carried pockets, a tactic known to enable convenient access to car keys—car keys, a tactic known to enable the driving of cars, the entering of homes and offices.

Others carried ideas, in invisible baskets, a tactic known to incite more ideas.

Others carried paper, a tactic known to enable origami, ass-wiping, face-fanning, petition-drafting, letter-writing, voting, littering.

Others carried tampons, a tactic known to enable convenient and tidy menstruation.

Others carried canvas shopping bags, a tactic known to stop tanks.

Others carried babies, a tactic known to be used to board airplanes early.

Others carried oranges, a tactic known to provide a handy and nutritious snack.

Others carried flags, a tactic known to incite patriotic protest and inspire impossible-to-sing anthems.

Others carried newspapers, a tactic known to incite reading and thinking.

Others carried shirts, a tactic known to be used to modestly cover nipples, known to be used to staunch the bleeding of broken skulls.

Others carried eyes, a tactic known to enable seeing, believing.

Others carried throats, a tactic known to enable swallowing, breathing, drinking milk.

Others carried teeth, a tactic known to enable biting.

Others carried ears, a tactic known to enable hearing the hiss of the gas canister and its clink on the sidewalk.

Others carried fingers, a tactic known to be used for pointing.

Others carried hands, a tactic known to be used for covering the head, the guts, the groin, against the rain of blows.

Others carried hearts, pumping and fluttering, a tactic known to push the blood into use and maintain life.

Others carried legs, a tactic known to be used for attempting to get out of the way of the falling baton.

Others carried Otherness—some easily, some bent beneath it—they could not put it down when ordered to do so.

Others carried away injured bodies, a tactic known to keep bodies from being further injured.

Others carried video cameras—pepper-spray-proof eyes plugged into long memory.

Others carried voices, a tactic known to enable talking, chanting, shouting, singing, testifying.

Others carried question marks, a tactic known to be used to ask questions.

Others breathed, a tactic known to be used to manufacture poisonous carbon dioxide.

Others carried bottles of water, which may not be taken through the TSA checkpoint—water, a tactic known to be used to slake thirst, to wet the voice for one more inconvenient accusation, one more adamant song.

Others carried hope, fiercely and tenderly guarding its necessary ember.

Others carried milk.

Others carried milk—tactical milk defensive milk mother's milk of human kindness—

And the milk was spilled, all the milk was spilled upon all the scalded eyes, and oh how we cried over it.

And even those milky, non-tactical tears were gathered up. We pressed them into shards, into service. We carried them.

Mark Faunlagui

BUT PARIS IS NO ALEPPO

tamarind
tamarisk

damascus
damascene

aleppo
alawites

they are
aslogging

through
each other's

first
borns

[funny—
not much

diff'r'nt
in 'murica]

TR Brady

HOPE AGAINST SUMMER

for Ally Lamb

somewhere, girls in Arkansas skateboard
cul-de-sacs. show-n-tell abs & sunblonde hair.

flex a little, give bracedsmile.
when brackets catch pull 'em off their cheeks,

smile bloody for each other. give
pen & knife tattoos, lines & dots on their ankles.

we hold match & needle
curse beneath bruise-breath, our boygirlhood.

all our dads—truckers or in jail or both—
build baseball diamonds, say, *son*,

build caskets outta guitar cases, whites, & whiskey
say, *you shoulda been a boy*. smoke another.

we wear our best on Sunday. sweat in pews, swear
we're learning to tie ties for future husbands.

•

we exist in trees & asphalt & our mother's prayers
against our t-shirts, cargo shorts, high tops.

we are there for the birth of sisters.
wipe the blood off their faces

give them chew & crew-cut & home.
beer from father's truck.

we give them catcher's mitt,
say, *you've made the grade*, slap her arm.

•

somewhere a girl is born
from ground buried remnants—

letters unmailed & collecting under first base,
backseats of Honda Civics.

in her own blood. in the moon.
in her father's fists.

in heaven.

i could tell you

somewhere, girls made fistbumps meaning forever,
a strong-armed solidarity,

but you'd have to see it: a jaw clench

a fist pulse

need for rest.

Alessandro Brusa

UNTERDENLINDEN—PART II

It's in our coats, it's hidden and it's buried in the skin we walk along these crowded streets.

It's the bitter almonds odor trapped in history, under the lime trees in Berlin and hitting the little lake in Central Park now it got all frozen over and the ducks have gone to hell.

It's rhythm but it's not discipline the rhyme I mime over those ridiculous lips and that dirty asshole I measure my life with, now that my scared siblings are stabbing frozen breath, for that is all is left.

It's time to go back underground while middle class sheep give middle fingers to fill the plates their masters take away from middle eastern brothers, while their homes sink into the middle age of mediocrity.

We do not talk: all we are able to do is entertain one another and the best entertainer gets the best job, swapping his images for our lack of ideas.

We've seen it coming, we've seen it coming again 'cos even some of us have never actually really stopped clapping. The APPLAUSE sign has never been switched off in their witless lives and that's all they could do: laughing and cheering, cradled in their *infinite appetite for distractions.*

: water smokes from across the ocean as your new tower soars our days.

Mx. Drinx

VICE PRESIDENT PENCE,

This Christmas, I grab you by the pussy and you love it. I pick you out at a party—one I am certainly not invited to but have no trouble crashing. I steal champagne. Its offer is implied, but the point is I steal it. Under chandeliers and portraits of pasts I've never found important, my polished claws find their place. They are transfixed, know which crevasse they are crawling toward. And it is perfect. The stuff emojis are made from. The kind of ass that doesn't need help from a high inseam, already the apple it ought to be.

You know year-round the indulgence a holiday can hold, can't wait to kneel at its edge. You are over-stuffed; I am always celebrating. You know it when I approach; you know it when I take hold.

You have no choice.

I am a star and I shoot to kill. This is the start of a meal. This is just the appetizer. You are par for the course.

Upstairs, I unpack to play, cite my right to the bare back as I open a brand new bottle of Gun Oil. You giggle a little into your elbow and agree. You are already ready— sturdy, bent over the bed. You ask for it all.

After, as I back away from the mess we have made, you ask if I want to see something funny. Before I can say *no, now's not the time*, your ass begins to clap— the wet webs with each toss of your back, a cat's cradle in cream-filled confession. In the shadow of your shoulder, from under your arm, I meet your eyes looking back at me, and above them, a smile so electric it feels like nothing less than freedom.

Erik Schuckers

PIRATE JENNY

I want you bed-sweet
with grease and victory.

I want you to know
that I know
what you will
not let me forget, that I
and this world are made
of your shit and phlegm.

I want only to be left
to get on with it, my slut's
remedies and mediation:
bleach, booze, bandage.

I want to offer
you my throat, my ass,
every tender slice.

I want to sing you
sweet as an icebox
wine, hot as kerosene.

I want to hold
you against a plague
of sirens.

I want to hold you.

I want to strip these poison
rags, to stride bone-picked
beneath the tetanus sky.

Money I want
money I want your
money. Give me
your money and shut
the fuck up.

I want to pry with
hungry scrub-knot fingers
every corner and cool
chamber of your body.

I want to suck your cock, and I want
bullets for teeth.

I want the burnt
sugar rumble of the blues,
thrum and thrust beneath
the devil's hand.

I want to burn
your ledgers of blood.

I want my dead
back, scrap skins tattered
flags of countries you
never
learned.

Emanuel Xavier

AMERICANO

I look at myself in the mirror
trying to figure out what makes me an American
I see Ecuador and Puerto Rico

I see brujo spirits moving across the backs of Santeros
splattered with the red blood of sacrificed chickens
on their virgin white clothes and blue beads for Yemaya
practicing religions without a roof

I see my own blood
reddening the white sheets of a stranger
proud American blue jean labels on the side of the bed
I see Don Rosario in his *guayabera*
sitting outside the *bodega*
with his Puerto Rican flag
reading time in the eyes of alley cats

I see my mother trying to be more like Marilyn Monroe
than Julia De Burgos
I see myself trying to be more like James Dean
than Federico Garcia Lorca
I see Carlos Santana, Gloria Estefan,
Ricky Martin and Jennifer Lopez
More than just sporadic Latin explosions
More like fireworks on *el Cuatro de Julio*
as American as Bruce Springsteen, Janis Joplin,
Elvis Presley, and Aretha Franklin

I see Taco Bells and chicken fajitas at McDonald's
I see red, orange, yellow, green, blue and purple
I see Chita Rivera on Broadway

I am as American as lemon *merengue* pie
as American as Wonder Woman's panties
as American as Madonna's bra

as American as the Quinteñeros, the Abduls, the Lees,
the Jacksons, the Kennedys
all of us immigrants to this soil
since none sound American-Indian to me
as American as television snow after the anthem is played
and I am not ashamed

Jose, can you see...
I pledge allegiance
to this country 'tis of me
land of dreams and opportunity
land of proud detergent names and commercialism
land of corporations

If I can win gold medals at the Olympics
If I can sign my life away to die for the United States
Ain't no small-town hick gonna tell me I ain't an American
because I can spic in two languages
coño carajo y FUCK YOU

This is my country too
where those who do not believe in freedom and diversity
are the ones who need to get the hell out

Karen Head

LISTENING TO MICHELLE OBAMA DENOUNCE DONALD TRUMP'S ABUSE OF WOMEN

Mid-October, work conference in Denver,
I'm just finishing one of those "free"
breakfasts at a Hampton Inn
served up on small round, too-low tables
topped with cell phones and room keycards,
thankful that the TV is set
to CNN and not FOX. Thankful,
that is, until the man sitting next to me
says to his friend, "Why does she always
have to raise her voice, be so angry?"
Every woman around me shifts in her seat—
except one. She is native American.
This is *her* country. She says loudly
to her bouncer-looking husband,
"Go get me another biscuit."

Something buried deep beneath
my whiteness, maybe ancient marrow
within the Cherokee cheekbones I inherited
from great-great-grandmother, Hester,
begins to leach out, surface.
Jostling his table, his hot coffee,
isn't hard with my woman's hips—
revolutions begin this way.

Rajorshi Das

AN ARMY OF LOVERS CANNOT LOSE

From largest to arguably the oldest:
Trumping its way,
Moditva in US.
For you turned out just the same—
Miming misogyny of powerful puppets.
Democracy indeed
Where majority strangles,
Cries out the hijab
Outside gated colonies.

There was RAF (Rapid Action Force)
At Delhi Pride few days back
Dressed in vigilant blue;
A timely reminder,
The first Pride was a riot.

A murderer here. A molester there
Perform their sacrificial rite.
The moment is ripe to strike,
To scream and dance.
As our ancestors said,
An army of lovers cannot lose.

Rossy Evelin Lima / translated into English by Gerald Padilla

EN ESTE PAÍS SIN VIDA / IN THIS LIFELESS COUNTRY

Que triste evidencia de estar viva
jugar con el óxido en mis piernas
y no saber cómo explicar sencillo
que vivo extrañando con las manos secas,
que sueño extrañando, una tierra de espejo.

Pero en este país de muertos
a la nostalgia le negaron la visa.
Ahora que soy una persona legal,
que me digan también
en donde tramito el olvido,
en el instante que me pienso libre
el recuerdo del hogar de dónde vengo
me hace caer de rodillas.

Me han dicho que estoy viva,
que siempre lo he estado.
Tengo 28 años y palpito,
aunque se me vaya el cielo
por estar fija en el sur,
ese lugar sin regreso;
aunque se me vaya el cielo
abrigando el destino
del mundo en el que había nacido libre.

Pero hablar de muerte es absurdo.
En el momento que yo quiera
me detengo a mitad de la calle y canto,
hablo entre soledades y espectadores,
y soy dueña de la soga y el látigo.

Cómo hablar de muertes
si vivo en la tierra del sueño americano.
Esta es mi casa,
aquí mis zapatos y mi ropa.

Such a sad evidence of being alive
playing with the rust on my legs
not knowing how to explain in simple terms
that I live yearning with dry hands,
that I dream longing, a land of mirror.

But in this lifeless country
nostalgia was denied a visa.
Now that I'm a legal person,
have someone tell me
where I can apply to forget it all,
the instant that I think of myself as free
the memory of the home where I come from
makes me fall on my knees.

They have told me I'm alive,
that I've always been this way.
I'm 28 years old and I'm a beating heart,
although the sky might leave without me
while gazing at the south,
that place with no return;
although the sky might leave without me,
sheltering the destiny
of the land in which I was born free.

But it's absurd to talk about death.
Whatever moment I wish
I stop in the middle of the street and sing,
I speak amongst solitude and spectators,
and I am the holder of the rope and the whip.

How can I speak of death
if I live in the land of the American dream.
This is my home,
my clothes and shoes are here.

La cadena en el tobillo no es nada,
no hace ruido, nadie puede verla.
Voy construyendo el porvenir
con el que sueñan muchos.

Hablar de esclavitud es absurdo,
estoy confundida.
No me dejan ver claro
estos dieciséis años de ceguera,
estos dieciséis años de saber
hacia dónde está mi casa.

Duele ser esta forma tibia,
medio viva,
en un país al que llegué
con el vientre cundido de esperanza,
                                la esfera pulcra
                        que nos alimenta de aire
hasta que encontramos el callejón
en donde tiran las sobras del banquete
al que no somos invitados.

¿Pero por qué hablar de hambre?
aquí lo tengo todo
en mi casa,
que no es mía,
que no existe,
porque mis ojos no la tocan,
no vuelven,
no se cansan de clavarse
en el cielo del recuerdo.

¿Qué significa haber vivido por 28 años?
Nada, no significa nada.
Mi experiencia es la ansiedad,
mi experiencia es la nostalgia
y el miedo de no poder volver.
Mi experiencia es ser fragmentada,
buscar mis pedazos

The chain on my ankle is nothing,
it doesn't make noise, no one can see it.
I'm building the future
that many dream of.

To talk about slavery is absurd,
I'm confused.
These sixteen years of blindness
don't let me speak clearly,
these sixteen years of not knowing
where is my home.

It hurts to be this warm being,
half alive,
in a country where I arrived
with a womb full of hope,
                                the unpolluted sphere
                            that feeds us air
until we find the alley
where the leftovers of the banquet
are tossed.

But why speak of hunger?
I have everything here
in my home,
that is not mine,
that doesn't exist,
for my eyes don't touch it,
they don't come back,
they don't get tired of staring
at the heavenly memory.

What does it mean to have lived for 28 years?
Nothing, it doesn't mean anything.
My experience is the anxiety,
my experience is the nostalgia
and the fear of not being able to go back.
My experience is to be fragmented,
looking for my pieces

y saberlos enterrados
en el fondo del río.

Estas son palabras simples,
mi experiencia es caer en el río
y salir a gatas hacia el asfalto.
Mi experiencia es ser puente
de un solo camino.

El mundo para mí
tiene los años que llevo buscándome,
perderme no fue mi culpa.

El mundo para mí es *Itzcuintlan*,
su orilla lodosa amenaza con el abismo,
pero nadie ve el abismo,
nadie conoce la angustia destructora
de cruzar serpentina para no ser escuchada.

El mundo para mí es *Apanohuaia*.
Pero el agua, aunque sea vida,
se pudre cuando se estanca.

and knowing they are buried
in the bottom of the river.

These are simple words,
my experience is to fall into the river
and come out crawling towards the asphalt.
My experience is to be
a one-way bridge.

The age of my world
is the years I've been looking for myself,
getting lost was not my fault.

My world is *Itzcuintlan*,
its muddy shore threatens with the abyss,
but nobody sees the abyss,
nobody recognizes the destructive anguish
of slithering across to be unnoticed.

My world is *Apanohuaia*.
But water, although it's life,
becomes putrid when it stalls.

H.K. Hummel

A BRIEF HISTORY OF THE LEER

At fourteen, I calculated the distance between myself and a chunk of basalt on an empty beach as a man wearing a shirt and nothing else came closer, closer. In a college dorm, I looked up from the boy I was kissing to see another boy watching and eating popcorn. At a gas station, I cut the engine, stepped out into a narrow circle of halogen light, and knew I was surrounded. Most days, I jog across the iron bridge that laces the river, past trucks that slow down as men flip a U-turn, pull over, lean out. Watching. Closing the distance. Muttering. Let me be clear: my beauty is unapologetically plain. I have any girl's ass and teacup breasts. I own four sweaters and three of them are beige. But, plain as anyone, I've loved each man I've loved with due abandon. This is different. This is about dingoes. Alligator waters. Smog under the skin. You learn to catch it in a glance, or in the turned-down mouth of that driver in the idling truck, or that nameless guy on the fringes of a frat party, or there, on that elected official.

Shittu Fowora

BEFORE THE WALLS RISE

those who saw the brits pother
Were darn sure
the yankees will pander
.... it's not armageddon after all—newsfeeds
are crimsoned, right
and for him, my sister voted.

of newspaperman mencken, i returned to the scrolls
and its poignancy strikes even harder.

for the absence of shogi in my head,
the headlines and newsbars are splattered
in red

another thing is, to hide
the voice of reason
trap a scarlet email,
screaming
blood red for brownies

we would never know what
folks behind the cubicle
are up to... to think, back home
we even
had a diddy of a seer

you're not asthma, how
could you tell a moan
from a whimper plea
from a grunt or a deigning
sigh?

you're an anathema
holding ballot
like a provoked man

with a pillow,
casting your violence
into her—America.

you're one who didn't
feature in this script
by and by, you'll get there,
hopefully, before the walls
rise:
for now sit back and enjoy
the movie parsing.

Kelila A. Knight

BEFORE BODY, BEFORE FLOOR

D said he would grab us by the pussy,

not knowing C had grabbed my pussy before.

grasping for the prize in the middle of the pit,

he reached inside and fumbled, claimed what he called

his *really big dick* was like nothing I'd ever had before,

his legs thwarting movement of my body

so I waited until he was finished, but that was not

the same as giving it up or giving up

his face and name, after telling the police officers

who doubted me (their faces in my memories)

not knowing my pussy would grab back,

C's hands had reached like a claw in an arcade

he used the classic grab and drop maneuver,

his force—I had never experienced this before—,

his hands restraining me against the floor,

so I could not, like sheath embracing sword, protect myself

the way I was taught to defend myself, and was not

giving up, I told myself—when I pretended to forget

that he had been a friend once because the officers

just wouldn't believe me—was not submission.

Scott Wiggerman

ESCAPE

starting with a Dickinson line (#508)

I'm ceded. I've stopped being theirs.
Now meeting dreams, not seeing theirs.

Unfettered of iron shackles,
I wasted life's days fleeing theirs.

Across the wide river I swim.
Is my freedom foreseeing theirs?

Out from shadows, into the light.
My own god, refereeing theirs.

In the clouds I soar from doctrine.
Choice is mine; disagreeing, theirs.

Sing the scars of my naked self.
My truth: no guaranteeing theirs.

Jocelyn Marshall

FOR THEM

Do not ______ this doesn't include me when
You do not get to ______ you don't
count, and she
does.
You do not get to sep
arate me from

that continues pumping blood through
these black-and-blue chambers
despite
wanting to free all blood
from the vessel
that's stabbed
too often.

They keep me wanting
to hear this beat—
speeding rapidly
with every footstep
in the battleground of
you.

Christine No

ELEVEN ELEVEN

My white friends are escaping to Joshua Tree in their BMWs and AirBnbs to drop acid and positive vibe away the election results; huddled around the moon around digital clock faces waiting for *eleven eleven eleven eleven* to make the world right again.

I on the other hand have not left my house since election night, and today am contemplating leaving bed at all—the dog whining at the door, haven't picked up after her, let her bark at the Rottweiler next door; oh big, dumb, Thor—

"Oh fuck it," I think, "one of us should be able to tell a big white dog to go fuck himself" as I imagine Brandy (my ferocious) does with each declarative bark. She's never been huge: a big medium, a tiny large maybe—always in that in between, little brown thing tucked snug into the bend in my knees, stubborn, immobile until I'm ready to get up. She's a pit bull, though, unwanted mutt returned three times her body broken, scarred and thin when we met on the sidewalk in Los Angeles: where we were both lost, it seemed.

We're lost again. Little brown unwanted and I; but not my white friends. They're flying in from out of town to gather over Trump's big win; to mourn, they say. But desert sunrises and mid-century modern furnishings, designer drugs. and hot tubs; waking up untouched by walls or bans or the fear of epithets strewn about their lawns, while hatred's free reign bombs bright imprints in the back of my eyelids, in my ever shrinking space—

They are artists. They'll wear onesies. They'll have coffee. Leonard Cohen. David Bowie. Hashtag #cuddlepuddle #notall-

They'll discuss the election, heads shaking. They will feel righteous in their indignation. They will stage a love-in, not a body of color amongst them. They will feel righteous in their indignation. The moon will rise. The drugs will kick in.

They will feel righteous in their indignation—

Raisa Fountain

BOUGHT AND PAID FOR

bought and paid for
husks of flesh clawing screeching
piling climbing clawing upward gotta gotta gotta
be the one on top
making sure all these other monkeys sit
underneath my asshole as my shit drips upon your crowns
celebrity death match
sardining those along the bottom
crushed by the weight of
everyone, climbing to the top of
the top of
...

winner winner chicken dinner
mr. george miller enjoys the victory of his chosen horse
fucker loves to kill blacks and rape girls
he is the enemy, his face just as prominent as this
disgusting plastic puppetry
plastered on all screens
digital code embedding your existence
he is coming for us
they are coming for us
cry, and drink your koolaid
rage as hard as you like
split a couple skulls and fuck up their system
revolution is dead
and so are we
they made sure of it

be calm
or dont
the divide EXPANDS
collapse is imminent
a few of us are bound to go with it
sacrifice yourselves

write some edgy existential words
circle jerk with some activists
or dont

none of this matters anyway.

CJ Southworth

AMERICAN OBITUARY

November 9, 2016

Call the undertaker.
Let him dig the hole among the trees
where no one will visit the grave.
It will be a silent burial,
the body never reported by the authorities
who gunned her down at the ballot box.

They will come for the statue in the harbor next,
melt her down for the copper,
recycle it into shining pennies
so you can keep your Liberty in your pocket,
share it with no one,
the way all freedom should be—
small and forgotten,
worth so little
you don't stop to retrieve it when it's lost,
barely notice that everything is gone.

Ina Roy-Faderman

COLORS OF AN AMERICAN

"When you mix the primary colors together, you get a rich, natural brown. Other variations give you a variety of muted red and yellow-oranges that can serve as the basis for many different skin tones."
–from Oil Painting for Dummies *by Giddings & Clifton*

I. Mother mourns in white,
I, black.
"You look like a ghost," she says.
Death makes ghosts
of us all.

II. Stylish girl.
Maggie sniffs, "Brown with black trim."
I say, "Just like me."

III. White bridal veil -
Mom whispers, "Like a widow."
I marry in red.

IV. Maggie's girl on my lap,
in the dentist's office. "No,
I'm not the nanny."

V. My son is golden:
dad's pink tinge, my dark eyes.
"Is he yours?"

IV. Then I speak.
They say, "Oh! American!"
A triumph.

Christopher Bakka

ARE YOU THE PRESIDENT?

"Have you outstript the rest? are you the President?
It is a trifle, they will more than arrive there every one, and still pass on."
– Walt Whitman

I will continue to check out
boys' asses & keep eating

pizza, I'll write until

I have got nothing
ecstatic to say

I will wake when I wake
& I'll sleep when I sleep

I'll smoke pot, have a drink
take a hike, call old friends
skinny-dip, explore caves
I'll admire the moon

I'll keep on fucking boys I want
& they'll keep fucking me

I'll read as many books
as I can read. I will continue to revolt

against my fascist friends
(I have no enemies except
self-righteousness & hate)

I'll go on playing with my cat
& give her too much food

I'll pet stray cats

I'll visit France again

I'll tip my local queens

I'll meditate on koans

Are you the President?

it doesn't matter
whether you are from the town of truth
or from the town of lies

although it's pretty clear
which town you're from

we'll take the right road
in the end

in spite of spite

we'll go on loving
long after you're gone

so I'm indifferent & proud

I doubt my doubt

& I will go on loving even you

Gustavo Hernandez

LA MIGRA

We see them in the fields like grasshoppers.
They're in the strawberry. They're in the lettuce,
and they analyze our bodies with their compound eyes—
        all blue.

The rows are avenues for solemn parades:
Green man, brown man, green man, brown.
The rustling of vine and leaf underfoot.
The thrum of the emerald eye overhead.

We're lined up in front of their trucks and their cages—
The tender, the sweet, the leaf, and the vine—
Some nervous,
Some veterans,
Some already settled and planning return.

Yuriko, the ranch owner's eight-year-old daughter,
looks on as her father strips us of our work boots
before we are dragged back to *our* dark-haired daughters—
before we are packed in a bright, rolling green.

Jonathan Mack

DEAR ANGEL

Wed.

dear Angel,
please understand that if I do show up I won't be any fun, I won't want to laugh or to fuck, and I'll be offended if anyone says it's all right. it's not all right. it's awful. it's awful and it's going to be worse, and worse for exactly the people who have already suffered the most. for example, the earth. so, you understand already that it's better if I don't talk, I'll just sit in the corner, on the floor, on the red shag rug, and read and drink wine. it's going to be way too much red wine and if you don't want to deal with that I don't blame you. I just want to sit in the corner, while you and your old deaf dog do whatever, so that I can read and drink and survive the proximity of pain, so that I can look up now and then, and see you, and the little old dog, and remember that love is still possible.

Kaveh Akbar

POEM TO A CONQUEROR

a groundwind wishes away
the dandelion

peels
and quarters the citrus

like wind
you come panting and aimless

bringing your own lumber
to warp and termite yourself

when you touch my face
you believe it is perfectable

you say
this is *perfectable*

when you move
you move like a carousel of flames

see: a row of broken chairs
in the pinerot

see: a petal
pressed between needle and skin

if the whole body were an eye
where would the hearing be

when I dream I dream like an ox
broken plow after broken plow

patience is a virtue
and virtue is easy

I only need to fear
the parts of you I can see

sam sax

11.09.16

the dogs don't know / the world / has eaten death / & become it
& i don't know / the world / is still turning / despite us / we chant
the names / of our dead at the capitol / as we've always done
we hold candles / in our upturned hands / we handle / our loved
ones / with a care reserved / for the last bread / in a dying city /
from the horror / that's known / into the horror / that cannot be /
imagined / give me one reason / to stay here / & ill turn right back
around / & around we go / the heart a planet / turning / you
who have survived / beyond reason / beyond reasonable doubt
& ballots / beyond country / or governance / or any god / you
who in the face of ovens / grow / how bread rises / in the heat

Joseph Harker

UNION SQUARE

And when they ask us, *where were you, what was it*
that you did, we will tell them

how we hummed beneath the surface, how we
set avalanches to slip with our whispers

for if nothing else, we have learned that revolutions
begin with the smallest of actions

like when one broken person tells another, *they cannot stop*
my love for you, writes it on a slip of paper to make it true,

sticks it to the wall where it is joined by another, and another
and another, until there are thousands,

monument of atom and sand grain, of blood cell and
photon, not called for but needed

like when our neighbors fall, and we reach down
to help our neighbors up

and when they ask us, *why*, we will tell them, *thank you*,
you have left us no choice but each other.

Mary E. Cronin

WE KNOW HOW TO DO THIS

We know how to do this—
To breathe in a house with no oxygen
to drive in a township where you run us off the road
to dance in a hall where you leer,
assess,
grab.

We know how to do this—
To speak in code
as you blunder and bluster,
smashing all the china
as you try to break us.

We know how to do this.
We meet eyes
We pass notes
We touch fingers
We laugh.

We are smoke.
We swirl around you
fill your eyes,
your nostrils,
your mouth,
as you flail
in vain.
We are an idea.
We are timeless.
You can't kill us.

We know how to do this.

YOU ARE THE RESISTANCE

ARTIST STATEMENT: SETH RUGGLES HILER

Progress is slow. Yet, change is quick.

Right before I put the final touches on "Fallen Progress"—the painting living on the cover of this journal—I had a Skype session with a choreographer collaborator of mine. I asked him if he thought our next project should be the one we had last spoken about six months before exploring the idea of taking to the open road, or if we should examine something less universal and more specifically of this moment in history. I said, "It seems everything has changed since we last spoke."

I picked up the laptop and showed him the difference between my painting from last spring and "Fallen Progress." They are both of figures with backgrounds of scattered colorful squares. But in the former painting the subject is hovering on the canvas. And my impression of this new one is more of a splat.

Between the painting of these two pieces, I took 100 days off from my studio practice and drove from Brooklyn to Cleveland to work for the Ohio Democratic Party as a field organizer. Not having any idea of what I was getting into, my goal was to simply help Hillary get elected in a key swing state. For the purposes of keeping this brief, let's just say I have never worked so hard in my life or believed in something so passionately.

We lost. It was a coup of decency. There are so many things that contributed to the outcome, and of course we continue to learn more. But, I have to be honest, I woke up on November 9th energized. I apologize that my first painting completed after my return is not that of hope, as I do have hope that this new era will create some amazing things. There will be a lot of strong art, that is already evident in the words of this publication.

This election has exposed the underbelly of hatred in this country. This was not a shock to all, as many people experience racism, xenophobia, homophobia, misogyny, classism, and more on a daily basis. I am hopeful that in this aftermath an awareness is growing—one of the imperative need for mobilization and action. If our political system is not serving us, we, the people, must influence. Find your cause. And flip the fear—everyone must directly (through phone calls, emails and yes, votes) threaten the jobs of politicians by letting them know that they will lose their power if they inhibit progress rather than create it. – SRH (www.sethruggleshiler.com)

BIOGRAPHIES OF POETS

A.A. is a poet and teacher of contemporary and traditional West African dance. She is currently working on several projects about the migration of humans and birds. Her work can be seen or is forthcoming in *The Seventh Wave*, *Maine Review*, *PUBLIC POOL*, and other magazines.

LIZ AHL lives in New Hampshire. Her most recent chapbook, *Home Economics,* was published in 2016 by Seven Kitchens Press. She is also author of *Talking About the Weather*, published in 2012 by Seven Kitchens in their "Summer Kitchen" series. Her second chapbook, *Luck* (Pecan Grove, 2010), received the New Hampshire Literary Awards "Reader's Choice" in Poetry Award in 2011, and her first chapbook, *A Thirst That's Partly Mine*, won the 2008 Slapering Hol Press chapbook contest. Her poems have appeared recently or are forthcoming in *Able Muse*, *Measure*, *Cutthroat*, and *Rappahannock Review*. She has been awarded residencies at Jentel, Playa, The Kimmel Harding Nelson Center for the Arts, and The Vermont Studio Center.

KAVEH AKBAR founded and edits *Divedapper*, where he interviews major voices in contemporary poetry. He is the author of the chapbook *Portrait of the Alcoholic* (Sibling Rivalry Press, January 2017) and full-length collection *Calling a Wolf a Wolf* (Alice James Books, late 2017). He was born in Tehran, Iran, and currently lives and teaches in Florida. In 2016, Akbar was a recipient of the Ruth Lilly and Dorothy Sargent Rosenberg Poetry Fellowship from the Poetry Foundation.

ELOISA AMEZCUA is an Arizona native. Her poetry and translations are published or forthcoming from *Poetry*, *The Journal*, *Cherry Tree*, and others. She is the author of the chapbooks *On Not Screaming* (Horse Less Press) and *Symptoms of Teething*, winner of the 2016 Vella Chapbook Prize from Paper Nautilus Press. Eloisa is the founder/editor of *The Shallow Ends: A Journal of Poetry*.

JOHN ANDREWS holds a BA in Writing from the University of Central Arkansas and an MFA from Texas State University where he was named a C.D. Marshall Creative Writing Fellow and served as managing editor for *Front Porch Journal*. He lives in Stillwater, Oklahoma, with his fiancé where he is a Ph.D. student in English and Creative Writing at Oklahoma State

University and serves as an Associate Editor for the *Cimarron Review*. His full-length debut, *Colin Is Changing His Name*, will be published in June by Sibling Rivalry Press.

ROBERT AULD is a senior at Salem State University. Poems appear or are forthcoming in *half mystic*, *Boston Accent*, and *The Merrimack Review*. With Sophie Klahr, he co-curates *Teen Sequins*, an annual online feature spotlighting younger poets.

CHRISTOPHER BAKKA lives and writes in Austin, Texas. You can find more of his poems in Issue 22 of *Assaracus*. Feel free to e-mail him at christopher.bakka@gmail.com.

CHARLIE BONDHUS's second poetry book, *All the Heat We Could Carry*, won the 2013 Main Street Rag Award and the 2014 Thom Gunn Award for Gay Poetry. His work has appeared in *Poetry*, *The Missouri Review*, *Columbia Journal*, *The Bellevue Literary Review*, and *Copper Nickel*. He is assistant professor of English at Raritan Valley Community College (NJ) and poetry editor at *The Good Men Project* (goodmenproject.com).

BRYAN BORLAND is founding publisher of Sibling Rivalry Press and founding editor of *Assaracus: A Journal of Gay Poetry*. He is the author of the poetry collections *DIG* (Stillhouse Press, 2016), *Less Fortunate Pirates* (Sibling Rivalry Press, 2012), and *My Life as Adam* (Sibling Rivalry Press, 2010). He is a Lambda Literary Fellow in Poetry and co-winner of the 2016 Judith A. Markowitz Emerging Writer Award. He lives in Arkansas with his husband and co-publisher of Sibling Rivalry Press, Seth Pennington.

ANDI BOYD grew up in south Louisiana, and she holds an MFA from Texas State University. She is a writer of both fiction and poetry, and her work has appeared in *Gulf Coast*, *Juked*, *Narrative*, *Drunken Boat*, and others.

TR BRADY is a poet from the Arkansas Delta. Her work has appeared, and is forthcoming from *Bombay Gin*, *Tupelo Quarterly*, and *Arkana*. She spends most of her time writing or making feminist cross-stitched patches with her partner at her favorite bar, ZAZA.

LACHLAN BROWN's first book of poetry, *Limited Cities*, was shortlisted and highly commended for the Dame Mary Gilmore Award. His poems have appeared in journals including *Mascara*, *Antipodes*, *Cordite*, and *Relief*. Lachlan is working on a manuscript of poetry titled *The Surface of Your Lunar Inheritance*, which explores his Chinese-Australian heritage. He teaches literature at Charles Sturt University, Wagga Wagga, Australia.

NICKOLE BROWN's books include *Sister* (Red Hen) and *Fanny Says* (BOA Editions). She was the editorial assistant for the late Hunter S. Thompson, worked at Sarabande Books for ten years, and was an Assistant Professor at the University of Arkansas at Little Rock. Currently, she is the Editor for the Marie Alexander Poetry Series and lives with her wife, poet Jessica Jacobs, in Asheville, North Carolina.

JEREMY BRUNGER is a graduate student at the University of Chicago. He was born in a cauldron of conservative bile and, once plucked from its borders, started reading Karl Marx. He hopes you will, too. He has written for *3 AM Magazine*, *Numero Cinq*, *Chiron Review*, and *Truthout*.

ALESSANDRO BRUSA was born in Bologna where he still lives. He has published one novel, *Il Cobra e la Farfalla* (2004), and one collection of poems, *La Raccolta del Sale* (2013). His second collection of poems, *In Tagli Ripidi,* is forthcoming (winter 2017). He's been translated into Spanish, French, and English. He's vice president of the organizing committee of the literary festival Bologna in Lettere.

JACOB BUDENZ (Jake Bee/Dreambaby) is a queer writer, multi-disciplinary performer, and witch currently pursuing an MFA in Creative Writing from the University of New Orleans. This wily witch's work has been published or commissioned by folks like *Glitterwolf*, *Polychrome*, *Hinchas de Poesia*, and The Baltimore Museum of Art. Most recently, the Baltimore Annex Theater produced Jacob's original adaptation of Bulgakov's *The Master and Margarita*, as well as an adaptation of Golding's *Lord of the Flies* written in collaboration with Madison Coan, Sarah Lamar, Sarah Jacqueline, and Rjyan Kidwell.

BOB CARR is the author of *Amaranth*, a chapbook published in 2016 by Indolent Books. In his writing life, Bob is currently working with Michael Broder as co-editor on the *HIV Here & Now* print anthology. Recent work by Bob appears in the *Bellevue Literary Review*, *Kettle Blue Review*, *New Verse News*, *Radius Literary Magazine*, *Pretty Owl Poetry*, *White Stag Journal*, *The*

Good Men Project and other publications. He lives with his husband, Stephen in Malden, Massachusetts, and serves as Deputy Director for the Bureau of Infectious Disease and Laboratory Sciences with the Massachusetts Department of Public Health. His poetry, book reviews, and upcoming events can be found at robertcarr.org.

KAI COGGIN is a queer Filipino-American poet and author living in Hot Springs National Park, Arkansas. She holds a BA in Poetry and Creative Writing from Texas A & M University. Kai is the author of two full-length collections, *Periscope Heart* (Swimming with Elephants Publications, 2014) and *Wingspan* (Golden Dragonfly Press, 2016). Her poetry has recently been nominated for the Pushcart Prize, Bettering American Poetry, and Best of the Net. She teaches an adult creative writing class called Words & Wine, and is also a Teaching Artist with the Arkansas Arts Council. For more, visit www.kaicoggin.com.

NICOLE CONNOLLY recently completed her MFA in poetry at Bowling Green State University, where she also served as the Managing Editor for *Mid-American Review*. She was a finalist in the 2016 *Sonora Review* Poetry Contest, and has had her work published in a few small presses. Currently, she serves as the manager for *Black Napkin Press*, a poetry-centric journal and chapbook publisher.

DEREK COYLE has published poems and reviews in the U.S., Britain, and Ireland; in *Irish Pages*, *The Texas Literary Review*, *Cuadrivio* (Mexico), *Wordlegs*, *The SHOp*, *Burning Bush 2*, *Glitterwolf*, *Skylight 47*, *Assaracus*, *Chelsea Station*, *RFD*, and *fathers and what must be said*. He has been shortlisted for the Patrick Kavanagh Award (2010, 2014, 2015), the Bradshaw Prize (2011), and in 2012 he was a chosen poet for the Poetry Ireland "Introductions Series." In 2013 he was placed second in the Bradshaw Prize. He lives in Carlow, where he is a founding member of the Carlow Writers' Co-Operative. He lectures in Carlow College.

MARY E. CRONIN lives on Cape Cod, where she writes in multiple genres, including middle-grade fiction, poetry, and essays. She holds an MFA in Writing for Children from Vermont College of Fine Arts. Mary teaches both English and Early Childhood Education at the college level. Her work has been featured in the *Cape Cod Times*, Shewired.com, and on WCAI-FM, the public radio station of the Cape and Islands. Mary is represented by Linda Camacho at Prospect Agency. Visit her website at www.maryecronin.com or on Twitter at @maryecronin.

BRIAN CZYZYK is a queer poet and writer from Northern Lower Michigan. A senior English Writing major at Northern Michigan University, Brian is an editor for NMU's undergraduate literary journal *Ore Ink Review* and works at the university's writing center. He has poetry published in and forthcoming from *Portage Magazine*, *Dunes Review*, *Sink Hollow*, *The Sandy River Review*, and *Indiana Review Online*. He believes in you.

RAJORSHI DAS identifies as a Queer scholar and poet from India. He teaches in Indraprastha College for Women, Delhi, and is invested in Queer politics as a means to reclaim the street.

MX. DRINX is an American anti-body, a newborn baby, and an I ain't shit witch. They find themselves growing caddy corner to confession, critique, and conceptual drag. In their day-to-day, they walk with R. Drake, an MFAW candidate at the School of the Art Institute of Chicago. They are the former host of Juniper Bends, a reading series in Asheville, North Carolina. Their work has appeared in *Assaracus* Issue 18, *WUSSY Mag*, *Crab Fat Magazine*, and their collaborative poetry zine, *Doing It Mostly Wrong*. Mx. Drinx hopes Mike Pence reads this and walks away a little wetter for it.

JIM ELLEDGE is the author of *Henry Darger, Throwaway Boy: The Tragic Life of an Outsider Artist*, *H*, and *A History of My Tattoo: A Poem*, which won the Lambda Literary Award in 2006. With David Groff, he edited *Who's Yer Daddy? Gay Writers Celebrate Their Mentors and Forerunners*.

MARK FAUNLAGUI was born in the Philippines and received a Bachelor of Architecture at Cornell University. He has studied with poets Geoffrey Nutter, Todd Colby, and Nicolas Destino. His poems have been published by Omnidawn's *OmniVerse*, Augury Books, and Greying Ghost's *The Corduroy Mtn*, and his manuscripts have variously made it as a finalist or semi-finalist in contests for Omnidawn, Augury Books, and The Song Cave. *On Some Hispanoluso Miniaturists* [1913 Press, 2017] is his first book. Mark is currently developing two other works, *Majnun* and *Embrujo*. He is an architect and lives in Jersey City.

MICHAEL G. FEDERSPIEL was born in Baltimore, Maryland. Months early. By cesarean section. At present, their poetics is intersectional, focusing on the foregrounding of marginalized voices. They are currently interested in the quality of human-ness, reconciling the divide between the interior and exterior selves, and sharing the schism with people. They are a graduate student of English at the University at Buffalo.

RAISA FOUNTAIN is currently 23 years old and from Carbondale, Illinois. She has been writing poetry since middle school but found her voice in early adulthood and pursued her craft through hosting open mics and performing in slam poetry competitions. She coached high school poetry slam at a Ferguson/Florissant high school in the St. Louis area in 2014 and was on the 2015 St. Louis Urb Arts Poetry Slam team. She went to college for American Sign Language and is currently taking time to figure out what she wants to do with her life itself in relation to her own happiness and activism.

SHITTU FOWORA is a lifelong fan of history and the power of scented words. He has recently been motivated by the winsomeness of birds and the wisdom of ants. Having been stung more than twice while attempting to lounge in trees to write verses, he now spends more time around PCs and electronic gadgets. At other times, he's in bed, not sleeping. A resident of Nigeria, his works have recently appeared in or forthcoming from *Inlandia*, *Sentinel Quarterly Review*, *Arc-24*, *Kitaab*, *Interviewing the Caribbean (IC)*, *Cha*, *Monkeystarpress*, and *Elsewhere Literary Magazine*.

YSABEL Y. GONZALEZ, a native of New Jersey, is also known for her performance poetry under the alias Ancestral Poetisa. She received her BA from Rutgers University, an MFA in Poetry from Drew University, and works for the Poetry Program at the Geraldine R. Dodge Foundation. She is also the Program Director for the BOAAT Writing Retreat and has been published or is forthcoming in *IMANIMAN: Poets Reflect on Transformative & Transgressive Borders Through Gloria Anzaldúa's Work*, *Wide Shore*, *Waxwing Literary Journal*, *Huizache*, *Acentos Review*, and *phati'tude Literary Magazine*. Find more of her poems and recorded performances at www.ysabelgonzalez.com.

TORRIN A. GREATHOUSE is a genderqueer, schizophrenic, cripple-punk from Southern California. Their work has been recently published in *Crab Fat Magazine*, *Glass: a Journal of Poetry*, *Ghost City Review*, *Calamus Journal*, & *The Feminist Wire*. torrin is the co-founder Black Napkin Press & an editor of *The Black Napkin*. When they are not writing or editing poetry, they are trying to survive in America long enough to earn a degree.

H.B.K. is a Jewish arsonist burning down the gender binary. They also enjoy writing and making comics. Contact them at gooseklein@gmail.com.

JOSEPH HARKER is a linguist-poet often found in the cities of the Northeast. His work has appeared in print and online journals like *Ganymede*, *qarrtsiluni*, and others. Someday he'll finish his manuscript, but in the meantime, he edits *Assaracus*. For more, visit http://www.jhpoet.com.

KAREN HAYES is a human being.

KAREN HEAD is the author of *Sassing* (WordTech Press, 2009), *My Paris Year* (All Nations Press, 2008) and *Shadow Boxes* (All Nations Press, 2003). Along with three colleagues, she recently published an anthology of occasional verse, *On Occasion: Four Poets, One Year* (Poetry Atlanta Press, 2014). Her poetry appears in a number of national and international journals and anthologies. She was the winner of the 2011 Oxford International Women's Festival Poetry Prize. She teaches at Georgia Tech, serves on the Poetry Atlanta Board, and is the Editor of the *Atlanta Review*.

FRANCINE HENDRICKSON is a writer. They belong to New York, and have performed at venues such as The Apollo Theater and Barclays Center. Their plays have been featured in Gotham's Young Writer's summer series, and they were a semifinalist for the 2015 Pablo Neruda Prize in Poetry. Their poetry has been published in *Nimrod*, *Pankhearst*, *ATOMIC*, and various other journals. Francine is currently pursuing a MA in Writing from Lenoir-Rhyne University.

GUSTAVO HERNANDEZ is a first generation Mexican immigrant, a writer, and poet. He is the proud son of Juan and Guadalupe, who gave more than they knew they had to provide a better life for their children. His work has been published in *Cactus Heart*, *Assaracus*, and *Word Riot*. You may contact him at Goldenarmor17@gmail.com.

H.K. HUMMEL is an Assistant Professor of creative writing at the University of Arkansas at Little Rock. Her work has recently appeared in *Iron Horse Literary Review*, *Booth*, *Flyway: Journal of Writing and Environment*, and other literary journals.

JESSICA JACOBS is the author of *Pelvis with Distance*, winner of the New Mexico Book Award in Poetry, an Over the Rainbow selection by the American Library Association, and a finalist for the Lambda Literary Award. Her chapbook *In Whatever Light Left to Us* was published by Sibling Rivalry Press in 2016. An avid long-distance runner, Jessica serves at the Associate Editor of *Beloit Poetry Journal*. She lives in Asheville, North Carolina, with her wife, the poet Nickole Brown.

RE KATZ is a genderqueer glitch performer. They have made three chapbooks: *Any Berry You Like* (iO Books, 2014), *an Author Collection* (Awst Press, 2015), and *Pony at the Super* (Horse Less Press, 2015).

COLLIN KELLEY is the author of the American Library Association-honored poetry collection *Render* (Sibling Rivalry Press) and *Better To Travel* (Poetry Atlanta Press). Sibling Rivalry Press is also the publisher of his acclaimed *Venus Trilogy* of novels, *Conquering Venus, Remain In Light,* and *Leaving Paris*. A recipient of the Georgia Author of the Year Award, Deep South Festival of Writers Award, and Goodreads Poetry Award, Kelley's poetry, reviews, essays, and interviews have appeared in magazines, journals, and anthologies around the world. www.collinkelley.com

CANDICE M. KELSEY's poems have been published in print and online publications, including *The Forum* (San Francisco City College), *13th Floor Magazine*, Tethered by Letters' *f(r)iction*, *50 Haiku*, and have been provisionally accepted by *Gulf Coast: A Journal of Literature and Fine Arts*. Candice is also the author of a 2007 trade paperback book (de Capo) which led to her spot on NPR with Diane Rehm. Candice earned her BA and MA in English from Miami (OH) and LMU respectively. She is an Ohio native who carves out life in Los Angeles with the help of her three children and many pets.

MITCHELL KING is an MFA candidate at Stony Brook Southampton. He was the recipient of the 2014 Jody Donohue Poetry Prize and his poetry has previously appeared in *The Southampton Review*, *Plenitude Magazine*, and

Matrix Magazine with work forthcoming at Rinky Dink Press. He is a Texan expatriate living in New York—he hopes someday to colonize the moon.

MICHAEL KLEIN teaches at Hunter College and Goddard College's MFA Program. His latest book is *When I Was a Twin* (Sibling Rivalry Press) and he is working on a new manuscript tentatively entitled *The Early Minutes of Without*.

KELILA A. KNIGHT is an MFA student at Oklahoma State University in Stillwater, Oklahoma. This is her first publication.

LIZ LAMPMAN is the 2016 winner of *Reed Magazine*'s Edwin Markham Prize for Poetry. Her poems have been featured in *Rattle*, *Lunch Ticket*, *The Missing Slate*, *Gulf Stream Lit Mag*, and other publications. She holds an MFA from Oklahoma State University.

ROSSY EVELIN LIMA is an international award-winning Mexican poet and linguist. Her two books, *Ecos de Barro* (Otras Voces, 2013) and *Aguacamino/Waterpath* (Mouthfeel Press, 2015) have received the International Latino Book Award. She has published her poetry in numerous journals, magazines, and anthologies including *Bordersenses*, *Acentos Review*, *Letralia*, *Periódico de Poesía UNAM*, and *Read Wildness* and has been translated to English, Portuguese, and Italian. She was a featured poet in the Smithsonian Latino Virtual Museum in 2015 and was invited to speak at the TEDx platform about her experience as an undocumented immigrant writer in the U.S.

ANTHONY LIOI lives in New Jersey, teaches in New York, and dreams of Rhode Island. His poems have been published in *Assaracus*, *Watershed*, *Blast Furnace*, *Green Humanities*, *The Dark Mountain Project*, and *Numinous*. He has just published a handbook of pop culture-based resistance, *Nerd Ecology*, with Bloomsbury Press. His Patronus is a greyhound.

JACOB LOTTER is a Junior at Westfield State University majoring in History with a Communication and Writing Minor. This is his first publication.

JONATHAN MACK was raised on a family farm in New Hampshire, but has spent most of his adult life in India and Japan. His story, "The

Right Way to Be Crippled and Naked," is the title story of an anthology of fiction about disability from Cinco Punto Press. He was a 2016 Lambda Literary Fellow in Fiction.

ED MADDEN is the Poet Laureate for the City of Columbia, South Carolina. A professor of English and director of the Women and Gender Studies Program at the University of South Carolina, Madden is the author of four books of poetry, most recently *Ark* (Sibling Rivalry Press, 2016).

JOCELYN MARSHALL is a PNW writer currently completing her PhD in English at SUNY Buffalo, and she has published and forthcoming work in the *Bellingham Review* and *Journal of American Culture*. She is a graduate fellow of the Northeastern Modern Language Association (NeMLA), an assistant director of the Riverrun Global Film Series, and a member of the *theory@buffalo* editorial board.

PHILIP MATTHEWS is a queer poet from eastern North Carolina. He is currently a Writing Fellow at the Fine Arts Work Center in Provincetown, Massachusetts; and formerly, Assistant Curator of Public Projects at the Pulitzer Arts Foundation in St. Louis. Poems have appeared in *Denver Quarterly*, *White Whale Review*, *Grimoire*, *Tammy*, and *Assaracus*, among other journals.

FREESIA MCKEE is a working poet. Her words have appeared in the *Huffington Post*, *Gertrude*, *Painted Bride Quarterly*, and Sundress Press's *Political Punch* anthology. She co-hosts *The Subtle Forces*, a weekly morning show on Riverwest Radio in Milwaukee.

MIGUEL M. MORALES grew up in Texas working as a migrant/seasonal farmworker. He is a Lambda Literary Fellow and an alum of VONA/Voices and the Macondo Writers Workshop. His work appears in *Imaniman: Anzaldua Poetic Anthology*, *Primera Página: Poetry from the Latino Heartland*, *From Macho to Mariposa: New Gay Latino Fiction*, in *Pilgrimage* and *Raspa* magazines, *Duende Journal*, *Green Mountains Review*, and *Borderlands: Texas Poetry Review*. Miguel is currently coediting the *Pulse/Pulso* anthology for Orlando.

LAURA RENA MURRAY is an investigative journalist whose longform work has appeared in *The New York Times*, *The Guardian*, *Al Jazeera*

America, *The San Francisco Chronicle*, *Philadelphia Weekly*, *The Center for Public Integrity*, and many more national and international publications. Her work has garnered numerous awards, including most recently the Carey Institute for Global Good Fellowship, the Rockefeller Foundation Bellagio Center Fellowship, the International Center for Journalists—Bringing Home the World Fellowship, and the Lambda Literary Emerging LGBT Voices Fellowship. Murray's poetry is often inspired by her reportage.

CARL NAPOLITANO is a recent graduate of Hendrix College where he studied creative writing and art and was the editor-in-chief of their undergraduate literary magazine, the *Aonian*. His work has appeared in *Assaracus* and *Cicada Magazine*. He lives in Little Rock, Arkansas, where he makes pottery and is an associate editor for Sibling Rivalry Press.

CHRISTINE NO is a writer and filmmaker whose work has appeared in the Sundance Film Festival, *sPARKLE+bLINK*, *Tayo*, *Columbia Journal*, and *Story Magazine*; and is forthcoming in *The Oakland Review*, *Apogee*, and *Nomadic Journal*. She is a VONA Alum, a Pushcart Prize Nominee, and the First Place Poetry Winner the 2016 Litquake Writing Contest. She lives in Oakland with her dog, Brandy.

CLARE PANICCIA was born and raised in upstate New York. She is currently a PhD student in poetry at Oklahoma State University, where she also works as an Associate Editor of the *Cimarron Review*. In 2016 she was a finalist for the *Indiana Review*, *Sonora Review*, and *Nimrod* poetry prizes, and her work has been featured in or is forthcoming from *Indiana Review*, *Grist*, *Zone 3*, *Crab Orchard Review*, *Best New Poets*, and elsewhere.

SETH PENNINGTON (Little Rock, Arkansas): publisher/designer at Sibling Rivalry Press with his husband, Bryan Borland; co-editor of *Joy Exhaustible* and *Assaracus*; new poems in *Lunch* and *Rhino*.

ROBERT ANDREW PEREZ lives in Berkeley and is an associate editor & book designer for speCt! in Oakland, where he also curates readings. He is an alum of the Lambda Literary Fellowship and a recipient of the Lannan Literary Award for poetry. His poetry has appeared in print & online in publications such as *DIAGRAM*, *The Awl*, *The Laurel Review*, and *The Cortland Review*, and has forthcoming work in *Vinyl*. His first collection, *the field*, was published with Omnidawn in their pocket book series. He is currently writing a movie about a divorce and wine tasting; it's a comedy. More at robertandrewperez.com.

BRAD RICHARD chairs the creative writing program at Lusher Charter School. 2015 Louisiana Artist of the Year, he is the author of three collections of poems, *Habitations*, *Motion Studies*, and *Butcher's Sugar*, and two chapbooks, *The Men in the Dark* and *Curtain Optional*. With Elizabeth Gross, he co-curates The Waves, a quarterly LGBTQ+ reading series at Antenna Gallery in New Orleans.

INA ROY-FADERMAN's work has appeared or is forthcoming in *Right Hand Pointing*, *Surreal Poetics*, *Pif*, the Tupelo 30/30 Project and elsewhere; Dana Gioia recently named "Elegy for Water" the outstanding poem of the *Richmond Anthology of Poetry*. A native Nebraskan of Bengali heritage, she received her formal creative writing training while completing an M.D.-Ph.D. at Stanford and UC Berkeley (philosophy). Currently, she teaches bioethics for Oregon State University, is a fiction editor for *Rivet Journal*, and works as a librarian at a school for gifted children.

SAM SAX is the author of *Madness* (Penguin, 2017) winner of The National Poetry Series selected by Terrance Hayes. His second book, *Bury It*, will be out on Wesleyan University Press in 2018. He's received fellowships from the National Endowment for the Arts, Lambda Literary, + The Michener Center, where he served as the Editor-in-chief of *Bat City Review*. He's the two-time Bay Area Grand Slam Champion, author of four chapbooks, + winner of the 2016 Iowa Review Award.

ERIK SCHUCKERS lives, works, and resists in Pittsburgh. His essays and poems have appeared in *PANK*, *The James Franco Review*, *The HIV Here and Now Project*, and *Clockhouse*, among others. His essay "Summer: A History" was anthologized in *Not Just Another Pretty Face* (Beautiful Dreamer Press).

RAY SHARP works in local public health in northern Michigan. His poetry collection, *Memories of When We Were Birds* (Red Dashboard, 2013) chronicles the seasons near Lake Superior. More at Raysharp.wordpress.com.

SAVANNAH SIPPLE is a writer from eastern Kentucky. Her essay, "Like it Never Happened...," was published on *Quaint Magazine*'s blog and was featured as one of 2015's Transformative Literary Essays by Sundress Publications. Savannah's work has recently been published in *Appalachian Heritage*, *The Pikeville Review*, *Southern Indiana Review*, *Still: The Journal*, and in the anthology *Appalachia Now: Short Stories of Contemporary Appalachia*.

CJ SOUTHWORTH is the owner and executive editor of Jane's Boy Press and the author of *And the Moon is Full Tonight*. He is a Pushcart-nominated poet and the winner of the 2015 Allen Ginsberg award. His poetry and fiction have appeared in *The Paterson Literary Review*, *Main Street Rag*, *Glitterwolf*, and other publications.

BREANA STEELE is a "liberal feminist killjoy" living in a dark red state. She earned her Bachelor's Degree in English from the University of Arkansas in Little Rock in 2014 and her MFA from Vermont College of Fine Arts in 2016. She is an associate editor for Sibling Rivalry Press.

GUY TRAIBER was born and raised in the sweltering middle-east and found love in the cold mountains of Europe. After a decade of traveling extensively throughout India and Southeast Asia, he is now pitched again on the soil of his youth. He studies and practices Chinese Medicine and hold a BA in Sociology & Political Science. He would appreciate your message at o13m@yahoo.com.

OSWALDO VARGAS is a Michoacán native raised in California's Central Valley. He is a former farm worker and studies History and Human Rights at the University of California, Davis. Publications include the forthcoming *IMANIMAN: Poets Writing in the Anzaldúan Borderlands* anthology and *Nepantla: A Journal Dedicated to Queer Poets of Color*, among others.

ISAIAH VIANESE is author of the poetry collection *Men and Music*. His poems and book reviews have appeared in *Blue Collar Review*, *The Fourth River*, *Lambda Literary*, *Moon City Review*, and *Rattle*. He is also author of a chapbook, *Stopping on the Old Highway*, and a book for kids. He lives in New York City, where he teaches writing.

SCOTT WIGGERMAN is the author of three books of poetry, *Leaf and Beak: Sonnets*, *Presence*, and *Vegetables and Other Relationships*; and the editor of several volumes, including *Wingbeats: Exercises & Practice in*

Poetry, *Lifting the Sky: Southwestern Haiku & Haiga*, and *Bearing the Mask*. Recent poems have appeared in *A Quiet Courage*, *Naugatuck River Review*, *Red Earth Review*, *Rat's Ass Review*, *shuf*, *Yellow Chair Review*, *Calamus Journal*, and *pnk prl*. He is an editor for Dos Gatos Press of Albuquerque, New Mexico.

EMANUEL XAVIER, an LGBT History Month Icon, is author of the poetry collections *Radiance*, *Nefarious*, *Americano*, *Pier Queen*, and *If Jesus Were Gay*, and the novel *Christ Like*. He also edited *Mariposas: A Modern Anthology of Queer Latino Poetry* and *Bullets & Butterflies: Queer Spoken Word Poetry*. One of the first openly gay Nuyorican poets, he has been a longtime gay rights activist, AIDS activist, and homeless youth advocate.

[YOUR NAME HERE]. Join us. Be a voice for the voiceless. Stand up to the bullies. If there's a separation, build a bridge. If there's a palace, be the hammer and the spray paint. If there's a wall, be the hands that tear it down. We are the resistance, and we're here to recruit you.

ABOUT THE PRESS

Sibling Rivalry Press is an independent press based in Little Rock, Arkansas. It is a sponsored project of Fractured Atlas, a nonprofit arts service organization. Contributions to support the operations of Sibling Rivalry Press are tax-deductible to the extent permitted by law, and your donations will directly assist in the publication of work that disturbs and enraptures. To contribute to the publication of more books like this one, please visit our website and click *donate*.

www.siblingrivalrypress.com

www.ingramcontent.com/pod-product-compliance
Lightning Source LLC
LaVergne TN
LVHW051006080826
845145LV00009B/2489